DISPLAYING FAITH

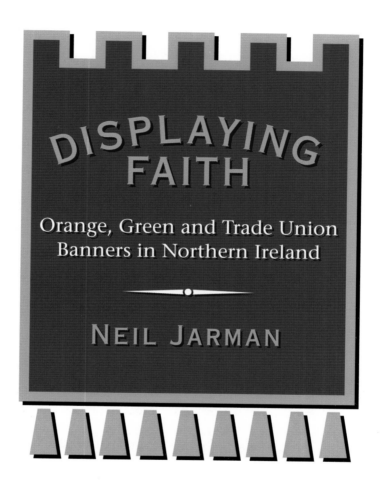

DISPLAYING FAITH

Orange, Green and Trade Union Banners in Northern Ireland

NEIL JARMAN

The Institute of Irish Studies
The Queen's University of Belfast

First published in 1999

The Institute of Irish Studies

The Queen's University of Belfast

This book has received support from the Cultural Diversity Programme of the Community Relations Council, which aims to encourage acceptance and understanding of cultural diversity. The views expressed do not necessarily reflect those of the NI Community Relations Council.

British Library Cataloguing-in-Publication Data. A catalogue record for this book is available from the British Library.

ISBN 0 85389 745 X

Front cover: (*top left*) Derry Division of the AOH, Derry, 1995; (*top right*) Shankill Road Heroes LOL, Belfast, 1990; (*middle left*) Belfast Branch of the Baker Club, ABoD, Londonderry, 1995; (*middle right*) Unison banner, Belfast, 1995; (*bottom left*) Warrenpoint Branch of the INF, Ballyholland, 1995; (*bottom right*) Sons of Elijah, RBP, Scarva, 1994.

Inside front cover: INF Branch St Peter Belfast, Ballyholland, 1995.

Frontispiece: Return from the field. Belfast, 1990.

Inside back cover: Pride of Ulster, RBP. Londonderry, 1995.

Back cover: (*left*) Billy Reid Republican Flute Band, Belfast, 1996; (*right*) Monkstown, Young Citizen Volunteers Flute Band, Belfast, 1991.

Printed by W&G Baird Ltd, Antrim.

Designed by Rodney Miller Associates, Belfast.

CONTENTS

INTRODUCTION

The popular political and commemorative culture of Northern Ireland is intensely visual. The summer months, from mid June to the end of August, are commonly known as the marching season, but this term fails to conjure up anything of the range and variety of the visual materials that accompany the thousands of parades that are held each year. These include such spatially anchored displays as the painting of kerb-stones and other street furniture, the hanging of colour-coded bunting and a diversity of national, regional and institutional flags, the erection of arches and the painting and re-painting of gable-end murals. The parades themselves are also resplendent with colour: in particular the hundreds of flags, banners and bannerettes that are carried and the uniforms worn by the many marching bands. All of these contribute to a highly visual set of ritual occasions. Much of this is so readily taken for granted that it is accepted as part of the summer events with little reflection or consideration. It is all seen as part of the local tradition.

In recent years there have been a number of publications dealing with aspects of the contemporary visual and symbolic culture. However, little attention has been paid to what is probably the oldest of these customary practices: the carrying of banners at the many parades. Banners are such a ubiquitous feature of the marching season that they are all too easily treated with a casual disdain and they are often ignored altogether. Orange Order parades have been described to me as a seemingly unending display of pictures of King Billy on a white horse. There is some truth in such a statement, Orange parades are dominated by banners of King William III. However, this does not do justice to the range and variety of subjects, styles and images that appear on the dozens of banners at the larger parades. A wide variety of images is also found on the banners carried by the other main marching orders and organisations.

This book focuses specifically on the banners carried at contemporary parades in Northern Ireland by unionist and nationalist groups and trade unions. It does so in two ways. The text describes how the contemporary range of banner images has been built up over several centuries. It looks at the history of banners and visual displays at parades in Ireland from the fifteenth century to the present. It draws largely on contemporary descriptions, often from newspapers, to trace the developments in style and subject matter among a range of different marching organisations. In particular I show how the body of images has grown steadily over the past two hundred years and continues to develop. As an extension of this I argue that the subjects on the banners are not a random collection of images or images chosen by chance, but rather that there is a logic to the range of paintings on display. The images reflect the interests of their respective groups and also serve to

Fig.1   King Billies at Larne, 1995.

help define that group. Orange banners display subjects related to Protestant faith and British nationality, but at the same time the sense of British identity is defined by the subjects on display. Similarly the Ancient Order of Hibernians display Irish nationalist images but their recognition as Irish nationalist images is in part contingent on their appearance at Irish nationalist parades. I show how these two opposing and contrasting identities were adopted in the late nineteenth century and popularised through such visual displays. The text therefore shows how contemporary political identities have been developed, established and maintained through a focus on one means of expression.

Alongside the text are over 100 images of contemporary banners, photographs that I have taken at parades across Northern Ireland between 1990 and 1998. These represent only a small selection of the banners that are currently on display but are broadly representative of the wider range of subjects and styles. Building up a comprehensive record of banner images is not easy. Many banners are only displayed once or twice a year. Most are on display at the main annual parade: St Patrick's day, May day, the Twelfth, Derry day, Our Lady's day or the Last Saturday. On many of these dates a number of parades are held simultaneously and it is difficult to photograph more than one or two of them. Taking photographs on location or during a parade can also create problems. If the weather is windy it may be difficult to get many good photographs. If it is wet and windy it may be impossible to get any as banners may not be unfurled. If the sun is at the wrong angle or is too bright it may also be difficult to get a good picture. However, the parades are still the best time to photograph the banners in their wider social context and the best opportunity for seeing new banners. I have found that the ideal time to photograph banners is in the hour before a parade is due to start when people are arriving and standing around after unfurling their banners. At such times it is possible to talk to people about the banners and to get them held upright or turned around to allow both sides to be photographed.

The photographs are linked to, but not purely dependent on, the text. I have tried to use the images to show the full range of contemporary subjects although these images are ordered in the book broadly in relation to their historical appearance rather than their numerical or symbolic importance. Some subjects have been used at parades for centuries. There was a representation of Adam and Eve at the Corpus Christi procession of the Dublin Guilds in 1498. They also appeared on a Belfast trade union banner in the nineteenth century and appear on loyal order banners today. There is no record of the how the guilds depicted Adam and Eve, but the banner image used last century is the same as the contemporary one. Clearly, however, the images mean different things at different times depending who is using them and how and where they are being used. The range of images represented by the photographs has to be seen as contemporary display and understood in terms of contemporary culture and politics rather than as an historical relic.

In the nineteenth century such displays were more widely used across Britain and Ireland – trade unions, friendly societies, temperance organisations, Sunday schools, social clubs and churches all had their own banners which helped to identify them at public parades. Visual documentation or preservation of these artefacts is relatively rare. Many banners were carried at parades until they were in too poor a condition to be used. Others were left to decay in cupboards or storage boxes, or abandoned when a lodge or division became defunct. Until recently there has been little interest in preserving or collecting banners. Few museums in Ireland have banners, of any kind, in their collections. They are difficult to preserve and awkward to display. Northern Ireland is unique in that the practice of parading with banners remains vibrant and one is not dependent on museums for an opportunity to see and record them. The contemporary banner displays are visually complex and many of the individual banners are beautiful objects in their own right. As such they are worthy of documentation.

MAKING BANNERS

The form and style of contemporary banners is an inheritance of the work of George Tutill who professionalised and monopolised the commercial banner industry in nineteenth century England. The company he began in 1837 is still making banners. From the end of the nineteenth century Bridgett Brothers of Belfast were the dominant painters and designers of banners for local organisations. Bridgett Brothers closed in the late 1980s and today banner painting is carried on at a much smaller scale, often as a one-man business.

Painters have a strong influence on the overall appearance of the banner and the primary focus of interest is with the two central images. A number of the most prominent images such as those of King William or the battle of the Somme, are based on original oil paintings which have then been copied, simplified and re-designed to fit the shape available on a banner. Other images have been designed by a banner painter at some time in the past and then taken up and copied by others: for example, many modern banner images are based on the work of Bridgett Brothers. However, there is no sense of copyright on any of the images. In many cases an old or damaged banner will be provided and used as a template for the replacement. As a result designs have become formalised and standardised and many of the images have changed little in style or content over the past century.

Some customers simply indicate the general subject they require and leave it to the painter to interpret their wishes by drawing on his experience or upon a range of past banners. But new images are also regularly demanded, a local building or a recently deceased lodge member is often included on a new banner. In such a case the painter may be expected to scale up from a photograph to make a banner image. All painters utilise a range of adaptable images; pictures from children's Bibles are valuable resources for banners of a biblical or religious nature. This is not as banal as it might seem since part of the painter's skill is to summarise complex stories and focus their meaning into a single salient event or a recognisable image. They must balance the need for a pleasing image with the desire to convey a specific message. The original image in a book or photograph is not copied directly but serves as the starting point from which the banner painter will interpret his customer's desires by repositioning or removing characters and working with the shadows, shading and colour to effect the best translation from one medium to the other.

The standard size of a banner is seven feet long by six feet wide and they are usually made of pure silk. The central image is enclosed within a frame, which varies from circular to shield-like in shape. A different image is painted on each side. Across the top of the banner is the name of the lodge or division along with its number. Along the

1

Fig. 2 Black Preceptory banner depicting the Garden of Eden. Note the smaller images of the Red Cross and Crown, the Dove and the Burning Bush which appear as the main image on many banners (see Fig. 8). The black ribbon is to remember a recently deceased member. Londonderry, 1995.

Fig. 3 A basic style bannerette. Rossnowlagh, 1997.

bottom may be an appropriate motto or quotation, or a reference to a geographical base, which is enclosed in a scroll form. Much of the remainder of the banner is covered with flowing, heraldic style floral or leaf designs. Bannerettes are small shield shaped banners, about three feet long and two feet wide. These are hung from a simple cross frame and carried by a single person. They are usually painted on one side only. Despite their size, the design follows the same format as banners with a central image, writing and heraldic scrolls, but they have less visual impact. District and county lodges in the Orange Order and Black Institution have

bannerettes rather than banners and many Apprentice Boys clubs carry bannerettes at the December parade.

In preparation for painting, the silk is stretched on a wooden frame to keep it taut. The central design is sketched on paper before being transferred onto the silk. A white ground is laid on first and then several undercoats added before the final image is gradually built up. Painting is done in stages and can take several weeks, as time is allowed for areas to dry before adding the next layers. Sometimes gold leaf or aluminium foil is used to add extra sharpness and brightness to the background of the images and the heraldic scrolls. This adds substantially to the cost but on a sunny day the banner will shine with an extra brilliance. Painters often work on several banners at once, with each at a different stage of completion. Once all of the painting is completed, a silk border, about eight inches wide, usually in a contrasting colour to the main silk background, is sewn around three sides, the top is edged with hoops from which the banner is suspended, and finally along the bottom a fringe and retaining ribbons complete the work.

On parade, the banner is hung from a cross bar, suspended between two wooden poles, which are topped by ornamental metalwork. Many Orange lodges use poles with a five pointed star in a circle; the Royal Black preceptories favour a compass and square; the Ancient Order of Hibernians (AOH) commonly carry a Celtic cross, while among the Irish National Foresters (INF) the Irish harp is common. Loyalist and nationalist organisations also allude to the military origins of this displaying practice by topping the poles with a small decorative axe head or a pike point. Two men are needed to carry a standard banner, supporting the poles in a leather harness worn around the neck. If it is windy, young boys will often be employed to hold the retaining ribbons to prevent the banner blowing freely. However, this turns the banner into a sail and often the banners are allowed to fly in the wind. Some of the older banners are made from canvas or some heavier fabric rather than silk and need a stronger frame. These banners are rarely seen on parades nowadays. At the AOH parade in Derry in August 1993, the Newry division paraded their banner for the first time in 25 years. It was considerably heavier than the common silk banners and as well as the pole bearers it required four men on retaining cords to keep it upright.

If the banner is protected from wind damage and carefully dried before it is put away it may last for anything between 25 and 40 years. Many

Fig. 4 An old banner belonging to the Newry Division of the AOH depicting a mass in penal times (see Fig. 13). Note the substantial wooden frame and extra cords used to keep the banner upright and the narrow outer trim on the banner. Derry, 1993.

banners are not treated with the respect required for this length of life. They tear while being allowed to fly freely in the wind, they are laid out on the grass prior to a parade, they are sometimes used to cover and protect band instruments at the lunch break and they may be rolled up wet at the end of the day. Notwithstanding this casual treatment many banners still reach an old age and many are brought out on parade despite being frayed, cracked and patched.

2

GOING PUBLIC

Before a banner is publicly paraded for the first time, it is customary to unfurl it at a dedication ceremony. These are local occasions but are advertised and reported within fraternity publications and some attract prominent public figures. The format varies from locale to locale: some take place in public, others are held in a church or other building; all involve a short parade as part of the occasion. In the weeks preceding the Twelfth of July, there are numerous banner unfurlings which helps focus attention in the build up to the big event.

On Saturday, 4 July 1992 a new Orange Order banner was dedicated and unfurled at Bessbrook, Co Armagh. Under tight security from the nearby military base, Orangemen gathered at their hall before parading into the village carrying their new banner (which remained furled) and accompanied by a local flute band. A crowd of perhaps 100 people gathered in front of an open sided articulated lorry trailer, which served as a platform for the officials. These included the officers of Bessbrook Purple Star LOL 959, the Bessbrook District Lodge and Orangemen from Belfast. They also included the local rector and the widows of the two Orangemen commemorated on the banner and the Rev Martin Smyth MP for South Belfast, then Grand Master of the Orange Lodge of Ireland, who was to be the main speaker.

Proceedings began with an introduction by the Master of the local lodge. He told people that it had been 30 years since the previous banner had been unfurled and this year had been chosen to replace the old one as Bessbrook was to host the Twelfth of July parade for the first time since 1981. The ceremony continued with the hymn *O God, Our Help in Ages Past*, a prayer and a scripture reading before the banner was unfurled. The new banner commemorated two local members of the Orange Order who had been among 10 men killed by the IRA at nearby Kingsmill in January 1976. It portrayed Joseph Lemmon and James McWhirter wearing their Orange regalia and between them the stone memorial bearing the names of all the men who died in the attack. The painting was underlined with the words *We Will Remember Them*. The unfurling, which took place immediately in front of the memorial depicted on the banner, was carried out by the widows of the two men and it was then dedicated by Martin Smyth. At this stage there was a pause in the proceedings as many spectators photographed the new banner. A second hymn was sung, and a final prayer said before a round of speeches was made from the platform. While the dedication speech and the introductions focused on the memories of the two dead men and the relationship between them, the Order and their Protestant religion, the final speech was an opportunity for Rev Martin Smyth to reiterate the Ulster Unionist political position. The ceremony ended with the singing of *God Save the Queen* while the public events

Fig. 5 Banner unfurled at Bessbrook depicting two local men killed by the IRA at Kingsmill in 1976. They are portrayed on either side of the local memorial to the event. Bessbrook, 1992.

Fig. 6 Hibernian banner unfurled at Toome. Although Hibernian banners have a basically similar form to Orange banners, they also differ in so far as they frequently incorporate other figures or symbols in the corners. This banner includes the symbols of the four provinces of Ireland. Note also the background images of a round tower, a Celtic Cross and the Rising Sun which are widely used on nationalist banners (see Figs 16 and 21). Toome, 1992.

concluded with the new banner being paraded up and down the main streets of the town by the Orangemen accompanied by two bands. Most people who had not already seen the banner were at this stage lining the streets to watch the procession. The proceedings took up the entire Saturday afternoon.

A similar ceremony was held in Toome in August the same year for the unfurling of a new banner for Drumraymond AOH Division in the grounds of the local Gaelic Athletic Association. It was attended by the National President of the AOH, Raymond McCormick, and attracted supporters from Derry, some 45 miles away. It was also a

mixture of prayers, hymns and speeches. The new banner was a replica of the previous one. The main image depicted the Maid of Erin receiving a Bible from an angel while the reverse portrayed a mounted warrior in medieval costume and a portrait of Canon John McMullan. In contrast to the Orange Order ceremony there were no political speeches at Toome, rather they concentrated on the events in hand, wishing the local district well and expressing relief that the rain had kept off. The banner was blessed by the local priest before the parade set off to display it around the town. The local division was accompanied by others from Derry and Hillhead, both carrying their own banners, and a number of bands. As at the Bessbrook ceremony, the majority of the people at the actual unfurling were members of the organisation, but large numbers of local people, of all ages, lined the streets to witness the parading of the new banner.

Early references to unfurling ceremonies can be found in relation to military regalia. For example, the *Belfast News Letter* of 20 July 1798 carried a report of the presentation of a banner to the Yeomanry Corps of the Fort Edward Cavalry, County Tyrone. The dedication speech concluded:

> As soldiers, you will assist under this banner, in defending the best of Kings, and our excellent constitution established in the Protestant Line, by our great Deliverer King William the Third, and now secured to us in the North of Ireland, it is to be hoped for ever, by the spirit and loyalty of Orange Men.

Similar practices among the loyal orders began to be documented at the end of the nineteenth century, at the same time as the banner iconography was being expanded and formalised. As the banners became more standardised in style and design, they were also becoming enveloped in ceremony and ritual. Among the earliest reports was the unfurling of the banner of the Sandy Row Volunteers on 30 June 1900. The banner was unfurled by lodge members and speeches were made but there was no religious ritual and the evening ended with songs and other amusements. The following year at a more formal ceremony the banner of Cleland Royal Standard LOL was unfurled by Miss Rose-Cleland with the words 'In

the name of God the Father, God the Son and God the Holy Ghost I dedicate this banner'. From this time on, formal opening or unveiling was rapidly adopted by Orangemen for all forms of public imagery, arches were ceremoniously opened and in 1913 one of the first murals at Dee Street, in east Belfast, was covered with fabric curtains prior to the ceremony.

In the early years of this century banners were usually unfurled on the morning of the Twelfth. Usually, a local woman had the honour of unfurling the banner, and she would invariably receive a pair of silver scissors as thanks. But sometimes local dignitaries unfurled banners which bore their own portraits: the future Prime Minister of Northern Ireland, Captain James Craig, unveiled the Killinchey Old York LOL banner bearing his portrait in 1905. Although local politicians were involved and took the opportunity to make short speeches these events do not seem to have been political occasions. Unfurling provided a public focus to view and admire the images and to commemorate the day in a local setting before setting off for the big parade.

After partition such formal openings become more clearly structured as public ceremonials. Arch and mural openings in Belfast often attracted Stormont MPs who took the opportunity to say a few words to the assembled crowd. Banner unfurlings were further ritualised by holding the event on or near to the anniversary of the Battle of the Somme at the beginning of July, rather than immediately prior to the Twelfth parade. The unfurling of a new banner became an event in its own right and at the same time linked the commemoration of the devastation and sacrifice of the war with the celebration of the continued vitality of the loyal orders. John Gorman's study of trade union banners *Banner Bright* records similar practices in England. He gives a brief description of a banner unfurling ceremony for the Northampton

Fig. 7 Unfurling a new banner at Rosslea, 1996.

County Committee of the National Union of Agricultural Workers in 1948. The banner was unfurled in All Saints Church during the singing of the hymn *Fight the Good Fight*. It was dedicated on the altar by the local vicar 'as a symbol of loyalty to God and our fellow men' before being carried to the local market place for its first public meeting. Surrounding the banner in rituals therefore appears to be both a longstanding and a widespread practice and it emphasises the significance of the banner both to the organisation and to the men who belong to it.

The unfurling ceremony is important because it announces the public existence of the group of men as a collective entity. Lodges can, and do, parade without any form of distinguishing regalia, but they are effectively invisible if they do so. Without a banner to display at public events the men are a nameless group of individuals, lacking a collective identity and lacking a history. It is the banner that displays the name of the body, its geographical base, its political and religious orientation and from its warrant number and sometimes from the image born on the banner, its history. The first public display of a banner marks the culmination of many months of work in organising ballots, dances, socials and collections to raise the money to pay for a new banner. The unfurling ceremony offers the members and supporters the first opportunity to scrutinise what will be the public face of the lodge for perhaps the next 25 years. It is a time for bringing people together and for celebrating the success of a collective effort, and although there may also be an element of tension and uncertainty as to how the banner will be received, unfurling a new banner announces a success. It may mark the appearance of a new lodge; be a symbol of a local resurgence, as with the ceremony at Toome; or the triumph of survival over local tragedy and adversity, as at Bessbrook; or it may simply signify the continued strength and success of a local group if the event marks the unfurling of a new banner to replace one that has worn out through age. Whatever the reason the appearance of a new banner marks a success and needs to be celebrated.

After the initial unfurling ceremony, a banner is rarely on public display. It may be on show on only one or two occasions each year. When the banners are paraded it is usually in the company of a number of others and among a large number of different images. These usually focus around a central theme or core image (King William III or St Patrick), which may be repeated many times at random throughout the parade, but the display always includes a number of images with no apparent connection to either the event being commemorated or the core image. Banners and images always appear in a random order and there is no sense of narrative. While many images clearly relate to the same period or series of events there is always a random intermingling of subjects at the parades. Not everyone may know the significance of each image, but the principal ones are well known and subjects tend to be restricted to a limited number of key themes. These limitations are enhanced by the constraints on depicting living people and when this factor is combined with the long life and the cost of a new banner, it means that it is impractical to use them for campaigning activities or to make contemporary political points (although these can be made by adding things to the banner: for example in recent years many Orange banners have carried a band of white fabric with the slogan *No Dublin Interference*). Therefore what is portrayed by the display of banners is a loosely structured history: a

commemoration and celebration of past heroes, glories and sacrifices displayed as both morality and exemplar to the living. Over the marching season one can see a number of variations of a celebratory remembrance, for the range of images varies slightly at each parade, and from year to year. As well as regional variations of emphasis within each organisation, loyalist and nationalist groups display their own interpretations of history as a feature of a wider political ideology. This means that the collectivity of parades, the marching season as a single unit, generates a number of varying histories which include contrasting and conflicting versions of the same events or periods of history. The banners are a visual representation of popular understanding of history and illustrate clearly the conflicting understanding of the past held by the two communities.

It has been widely stated that the past has a particular significance in the north of Ireland, but surprisingly few of the myriad events of Irish history are publicly commemorated in any way. Many minor events and lesser personalities of Irish and Ulster history remain in the public eye solely as a result of being displayed on the banners. It is only on the larger occasions that the wide range of historical events and personalities are gathered together and the full sweep of history laid out for display for those members of the public who choose to watch. Members of the parading organisations themselves see very few of the banners on display; most follow their own banners year after year and only get brief glimpses of those that are carried immediately in front of their own banner. The banner displays therefore demand and assume the presence of an observer. But the spectator is rarely a neutral or disinterested onlooker, but rather is part of the broader silent majority of support, and part of the wider community of faith.

Most of the histories that are displayed are based around the one or two key events or figures which enable the viewer to locate the secondary subjects within a more general but clearly positioned historical schemata. The apparently random order of the images and the lack of a coherent narrative are an important means of equalising events of apparently vastly different significance. It also helps condense several hundred years of history by denying and refusing any sense of temporal order or passage. The juxtaposition of events such as the battle of the Boyne with the battle of the Somme, or individuals such as St Patrick and Daniel O'Connell, creates an equality of value between events of the recent past, still recalled by the living and remembered in oral histories and those of the distant almost mythological past. History and time become condensed into a single concept of the past, an entity constructed of categories of events: sacrifice, martyrdom, betrayal, faith. This past is not ended but continues to structure the feelings, expectations and fears of those acting in the present. The past can also be added to and extended with the commemoration of new local heroes whose modest faith and sacrifices are publicly recalled each year, as their images are paraded through the streets of Ulster.

THE USE OF COLOUR

The focus of this study is on the variety of images portrayed on the banners, their historical context, local relevance and contextual meanings, but colour can, and often is, a bearer of symbolic meanings. The colours of the fabric may appear to be of little importance in comparison to the images they bear, but one is always aware of the importance of colour symbolism in Ireland. Nationalist and unionist banners utilise distinct colours and colour combinations for their banners. Whilst these may appear to be obvious, there is no natural relationship between political allegiance and colour – it is always historically structured. The wider range and variety of colours used by the trade unions on their banners illustrates this point.

Each banner has two main coloured areas: the main piece of fabric, which carries the images and decorations, and the outer border. In most cases these two parts of the banner are of different colours. The Hibernians and Foresters restrict themselves almost entirely to the use of green for the central portion and orange for the border. Green and orange are easily recognised as two of the colours of the tricolour of the Irish Republic and green has long been the colour of Nationalist Ireland. Green flags were carried during the United Irishmen rebellion in 1798 and at many of the large demonstrations held as part of Daniel O'Connell's repeal campaign in the 1840s. It is unclear when and why green was adopted as the Irish colour but it has had a symbolic significance for many centuries as the colour used to represent St Brigid. Jeanne Sheehy notes that the seventeenth century traveller Thomas Dinely recorded in his journal that the common people wore the green shamrock as their emblem on St Patrick's day, although blue was the official colour of Ireland. Blue retained this status until the end of the nineteenth century.

According to Hayes-McCoy the flags incorporating green and orange first appeared during Daniel O'Connell's repeal campaign and was also used widely by the Young Irelanders and was flown during the 1848 rising. The tricolour form of the flag was probably influenced by the French example. However, orange was only incorporated into the Irish national colours for the first time in 1916 when the tricolour was raised over the GPO in Dublin beside the national green flag with a gold harp, at the start of the Easter Rising. The tricolour symbolises the idealised unity of the two dominant groups within a united Ireland. White, the third element of the tricolour, has no place on the banners. It may be thought that white functions simply as a bridge to link and unite the orange and the green; but white has had a wide historical use in Ireland. In the late eighteenth century the white flag was the emblem of the Defenders and was carried by some of the rebels in 1798. Earlier still it was the colour of another of the agrarian bands, the Whiteboys and before that the Jacobites. However, the lack of white as a main colour on any of the banners suggests that these historical meanings have little resonance today.

Turning to the loyal order displays, one is immediately aware of the use of a much greater range of both colours and colour combinations. The most common ones are orange, purple, crimson and black, in addition, blue, green, red and white are also used. Although the main organisations have fraternal affiliations and overlapping membership, few of these colours are used by all of the orders. Black Preceptory banners scarcely use orange, purple or crimson; few Orange Order banners use black and only a small number use crimson; few Apprentice Boys banners use black or purple although orange is widely used. Even the secondary colours do not overlap very much, blue is widely used by the Orange Order and the Apprentice Boys but not by the Black who alone use green frequently. Only red features prominently on all three groups of banners. Some of these colours have an obvious significance, the importance of others is less clear.

The most prominent loyalist colour is orange, which has come to signify the Ulster Protestant population en masse. Its origin and significance derives from William III whose ancestral seat was not in his Dutch homeland, but in the French town of Orange in the Rhone valley. In public decoration orange is frequently combined with purple, the colour of the higher but least public stage of Orangeism, the Royal Arch Purple Chapter. It is also a colour with long associations in western symbolism with wealth, luxury and status dating back to Roman times.

Black nearly always has a negative symbolic meaning in western and Christian traditions, but in this case the point of reference appears to be to the history or claimed ancestry of the loyal order. The roots of the Royal Black Institution are said to

Fig. 8 The Red Cross and Crown is a widely used image on Black banners, which explicitly links royal status with Protestant faith, here symbolised by the open Bible. Similar banners often include the motto *No Cross, No Crown*, which reaffirms the message of the image. Black Preceptories use the term 'encamped' to describe their home base. Scarva, 1993.

derive from medieval orders of chivalrous knights, such as the Knights of Malta or the Knights of St John who were often referred to as Black Knights from the colour of the robes they wore. In this case black symbolises human frailty and mortality. Crimson, the dark red colour of the Apprentice Boys, comes from Mitchelburne's 'bloody flag' which was raised on the steeple of St Columb's Cathedral during the siege of Derry as an act of defiance and symbolises the blood shed by the defenders.

Red is also commonly used for Apprentice Boys banners, possibly as an alternative to crimson.

It is also widely used on the Black banners, with a red border and a black centrepiece one of the most popular combinations. Red has significance as two of the internal degrees within the Black Institution, the highest degree being the Red Cross. The Red Cross is also featured as an image on several banners, the imagery here within the context of a wide range of religious imagery alluding specifically to Christ's crucifixion. Red also has particular reference to Ulster through the symbol of the red hand. Historically the symbol derives from the coat of arms of the earls of Tyrone but it also has a mythological symbolism. In the tale two warriors each sought to claim possession of Ulster by racing to be the first to reach land. The losing man cut off his own hand and threw it over the head of his rival to ensure victory. All three meanings therefore reiterate a willingness to shed blood as an act of sacrifice to achieve one's aims, a theme widely referred to in more explicit terms in the banner images.

Blue is widely used on both Orange and Apprentice Boys banners but is rare on Black banners. Patrick Macrory notes that when William of Orange landed at Torbay he unfurled a blue banner inscribed *For the Protestant Religion and Liberty*. The frequent use of blue on Orange Order banners, particularly in combination with orange, most probably derives from this association. It also suggests a reference to William as monarch and authority, widespread in such terms as blue-blooded and royal blue, and it creates a link with its earlier usage as the official state colour for Ireland noted above. Finally, blue was widely used by the Freemasons and the combination of orange and blue once suggested close links between the two bodies.

The Orange Order and the Apprentice Boys both use white, yet there are few obvious local symbolic connotations. The only instance where white has a central role is in regard to King William's horse when, from historical precedent, it would seem to emphasise purity and goodness. One other historical reference point was during the siege of Derry where wearing white armbands was a symbol of the determination to continue the siege. This might explain why the crimson sash of the Apprentice Boys is frequently fringed with white. Green is not widely used except by the Royal Black Institution where the Royal Green is one of the degrees of membership within the institution. The colour is so widely recognised as the Irish nationalist colour that it is difficult to establish any meaningful Protestant symbolic values. But one should acknowledge that some Ulster Protestants accept themselves as Irish as well as British, although for most, this is not an identity based on any sense of shared cultural values, but rather on contesting the ownership and interpretation of the past. In 1970 William McGrath, founder of the paramilitary group Tara, formed an Orange Lodge named Ireland's Glory and whose banner carried a map of Ireland, the heraldic shields of Belfast, Derry, Dublin and Cork and the motto *Occupy till I Come* along with other inscriptions in Irish. However, such deviations from the norm have not been repeated.

Colour therefore is an important facet of the visual displays. Many of the colours have a clear symbolic resonance which have been built up over the centuries until they appear so obvious that we consider the associations natural. In similar fashion the images that are depicted on the banners appear readily associated with either nationalism or unionism. But they too have no natural relationship with a contemporary political ideology. The remainder of this study will explore how the broad collections of images that appear on parades have been built up slowly over many decades.

4

EARLY HISTORY OF PARADES AND DISPLAYS

Celebratory and commemorative parades have been documented as a part of Irish social, religious and political life since the late fifteenth century when the annual procession of the guilds through Dublin was recorded in some detail. In the centuries that followed parades were adopted by a diverse range of bodies to display their public existence, their authority, their faith, their strength of support and either their loyalty or opposition to crown and state.

The trade and merchant guilds were prominent in many Irish towns until the early nineteenth century. They were responsible for regulating trade and commerce and more generally for electing the town corporation. In Dublin the guilds held numerous public processions: Corpus Christi and St George's day parades were the most important pageants until the early seventeenth century. Thereafter annual church parades and the Riding of the Franchises, to mark the boundaries of municipal authority, were the most prominent displays of guild wealth and authority. The report of the Corpus Christi procession through Dublin in 1498, whose practice was set down in 'an olde law', records how different guilds performed elaborate costumed mysteries at various locations across the city. Each guild enacted a story which was related to their patron saint or recreated an episode from the Bible. Among the stories featured were those of Adam and Eve, Noah, Abraham and Isaac and Moses from the Old Testament, and the Three

Fig. 9 Adam and Eve being cast out of Eden has served as a powerful symbol in public events since at least the fifteenth century. As well as the moral of the tale they have also served as patrons for various tailors' guilds and unions. Bangor, 1993.

Kings, Christ in his Passion, and the Twelve Apostles from the New Testament. Alongside these Biblical figures were representations of historical figures, such as 'Arthure, with knightes' and St

Fig.10 Abraham's willingness to sacrifice his son Isaac is held up as an example of true faith. Bangor, 1993.

own distinctive colours and members wore similar coloured cockades in their hats. Each guild also carried a banner, which depicted their patron saint, the coat of arms of the town or a combination of both. The few surviving examples of guild banner designs all date from the nineteenth century, but the images on them have their roots in the biblical themes that had once been physically enacted at the Corpus Christi pageants.

During the seventeenth century, the officers of state at Dublin Castle established annual church parades to mark the Gunpowder Treason Plot of 1605 and the Rebellion of 1641. These were solemn occasions of 'the great and the good' and, although popular celebrations and processions were encouraged to mark a number of royal anniversaries during the 1670s, it was only after the Williamite succession that more elaborate state displays were held. A formal procession to mark the victory at the Boyne was held on King William's birthday, 4 November, in 1690 and this was soon adopted as an annual event. Similar parades were held on a range of royal birthdays and anniversaries in the years that followed but 4 November remained the most prominent public celebration at this time. Contemporary reports of the proceedings suggest that initially at least, the parades were seen as professions of loyalty and support for the monarchy rather than a celebration of the military victories of 1688–91. During the Hanoverian period such displays of loyalty were further encouraged, and the proliferation of royalist parades and demonstrations reduced the significance of the Williamite anniversaries, although state support for these continued into the nineteenth century.

George. The leading members of the guilds processed on horseback, while the mysteries were performed on movable stages. The whole event was accompanied by numerous musicians and must have been a considerable spectacle.

Throughout the seventeenth century, emphasis was placed on the responsibility of the guilds for the defence of Dublin. Processions were held on Easter Monday (Black Monday) to commemorate a thirteenth century battle on the outskirts of the city and on this occasion guild members were expected to undergo military exercises under penalty of a fine. However, by the early eighteenth century the main public display by the guilds was at the Riding of the Franchises. On these occasions each guild carried a flag in its

The guild and state processions were relatively discrete displays of wealth, prestige and authority. The lower orders did not participate in the parades but were restricted to the role of spectators. In fact parading does not seem to have been widely established in the popular imagination as an appropriate means of public celebration at this time. Instead, people gathered at bonfires, watched firework displays and ate and drank the night away. It was only towards the middle of the eighteenth century that parading became a more widespread social and political activity and a wider range of social groups began to imitate the upper class practices and hold regular parades. The Freemasons held their first parade shortly after the formation of a Grand Lodge in Dublin when they processed through the city on the day of their patron, St John's day (24 June) 1725. Hereafter the Freemasons held occasional parades through Dublin, while during the 1730s and 1740s Masonic processions were recorded as far afield as Coleraine and Cork. In this same period several of the journeymen associations began to copy their masters in the guilds. The associations of tailors, shoemakers, draymen, chimney sweeps and others held individual parades to church on their patron's days, and they also came together for much larger scale gatherings of loyalty and to honour the king. While most reports emphasise such parades in Dublin and Cork, the northern workers also joined in with this growing custom. In the 1740s and 1750s the weavers in Belfast and Lurgan displayed their loyalty by marching in their local areas to mark military victories over the French and the defeat of the Jacobites.

It was around this time that popular public processions to commemorate the Williamite victories also began to be established as regular events in Dublin. The initiative seems to have been taken by the Boyne Society, one of a number of such loyal clubs, when it marked the fiftieth anniversary of the battle by parading to church on 1 July 1740 and afterwards marched through the city to the accompaniment of music and drums and the firing of guns and pistols. With the Aughrim Society adopting a similar form of

Fig.11 The battle of Aughrim, fought on 12 July 1691, was the last major conflict of the Williamite wars. It was commemorated by parades in Dublin and elsewhere through the eighteenth century. Antrim, 1995.

celebration on 12 July, Williamite parades became a central feature of Dublin's public calendar. Parades gradually became accepted as the most appropriate means of commemorating these anniversaries, although it was not until 1775 that the first such Williamite parade was recorded in Ulster. On 12 July that year the Protestant gentlemen of Tandragee paraded through the town 'preceded by a band of music; with flags etc' having first decorated the market house with an orange and blue flag bearing the motto *Protestant Interest*.

In general, parading was not used extensively for political protest until later in the century, although supporters of the Jacobite cause provoked some consternation by parading in

Dublin on the birthday of the Pretender in 1724 and for a number of years thereafter. The rural population did sometimes assemble in large numbers in support of their grievances, but usually this was only done under cover of darkness, although large rural gatherings on holy days or at holy wells were often treated with suspicion and concern by the authorities. However, there is little to indicate whether such assemblies were anything other than bona fide religious gatherings. More formal and overt political demonstrations were only rarely recorded. One prominent example was the Oakboys who marched the roads of counties Armagh, Monaghan and Tyrone during the few brief weeks of June and July 1763 when they mounted their campaign against rural tax increases. The Oakboys probably represent the earliest example of members of the Protestant community parading in support of their political demands.

These diverse popular parades all adopted a broadly similar form which drew on the styles of both the guild and state displays. Two elements were prominent in all these events: music and a range of visual displays. The music was often an attraction in its own right. Even when an anniversary was just being celebrated at a bonfire or in a tavern, musicians were usually present. But the music also helped to keep the marchers in some kind of order and it served to announce its imminent arrival to potential spectators, while on occasions it could also serve as a warning to those who wished to avoid the spectacle. Flute and drums were the main accompaniment to a parade, but horns, fiddles and bagpipes were also used.

Visual displays were more varied and could often be very elaborate. The more formally constituted bodies had a distinctive uniform dress and personal regalia, the Freemasons for instance wore decorated aprons and white gloves and the Williamite clubs also seem to have worn distinctive uniforms. At more informal gatherings people simply donned coloured ribbons and cockades to indicate their support. Floral emblems were also widely used: the Aughrim Society wore 'Orange cockades and green boughs' on their earliest parades and by 1750 the Orange lily was being worn for the Williamite celebrations. The Jacobite supporters did likewise and wore either white ribbons or white roses, while the Oakboys decorated their houses and their coats with oak leaves.

Flags, banners and effigies were also frequently carried, but there is little in the way of detailed information outside the guild traditions. Sometimes effigies are noted, as in the example of the bricklayers and masons who paraded through Dublin to mark the 'Solemnization of the Proclamation Day of his late Majesty of Happy Memory' in August 1728 carrying a model of a 'King Solomon Figure at their front and the Famous Temple finely adorn'd in miniature carried before him'. More commonly, however, reports simply refer to the carrying of 'flags and colours' and offer little in the way of detail. A letter in the *Cork Evening Post* in July 1763, describing the activities of the Oakboys, notes that they paraded in companies 'with each having a standard, or colours displayed'. Similarly the Lurgan weavers, who paraded to celebrate the defeat of the Jacobites at Culloden in 1753, marched with 'colours belonging to their society'. In neither case is any further detail offered although one might speculate that the weavers, at least, might have followed in the guild tradition and displayed references to their patron. Apart from the description of the orange and blue flag at Tandragee, it is not until the rise of the Volunteer movement in the late 1770s that we have evidence of more elaborate banners and flags.

Fig.12 (*opposite*) Like Adam and Eve, Solomon has served as a symbol for centuries. The Black banners emphasise his biblical importance whereas eighteenth century masons used him as a patron figure. The mason's square and compass is also an important Black symbol. Londonderry, 1995.

5

THE VOLUNTEERS

In the eighteenth century holding parades was largely an urban custom in which Dublin took the lead as the middle class organisations adopted aristocratic and state practices. Outside the capital and a few larger towns, parading was a much more occasional occurrence. Most commemorations of events such as the Gunpowder Treason Plot or the 1641 Rebellion were confined to church services, and celebrations of the Williamite victories were centred on the tavern, the dining room or the bonfire. Although public commemorations became more widespread as the century progressed, they remained respectable events. They were an exercise of privilege and demonstrations of wealth, faith and loyalty. The lower classes were rarely able to take part in the processions except when they mobilised as an expression of loyalty, and members of the Catholic community were largely excluded from participating in public life by the Penal Laws. Nevertheless, the example of the Oakboys illustrates that public processions could readily be utilised as part of more overt political demands and the practice of holding regular formal parades in conjunction with a political campaign was extended and consolidated by the Volunteers between 1777 and 1792.

The first Volunteer company was raised in Belfast on St Patrick's day 1777 in response to the harrying of shipping in Belfast Lough by American privateers during the American War of

Fig.13 A common version of the Penal Mass (see Fig. 4) depicts a snow-covered landscape and British soldiers approaching in the distance. Note the shamrock designs and the AOH symbol of fraternity in the upper left and lower right corners. Toome, 1995.

Independence. To aid the war effort British troops had been withdrawn from Ireland and this in turn raised fears of a French invasion. To counter their concerns the Protestant middle and upper classes organised into Volunteer companies and began military training. Volunteering became so popular that by 1780 there were over 60,000 men enrolled in companies across Ireland. With the ending of the threat of invasion, the Volunteers turned their attention to political matters. In particular they supported the growing demands for greater parliamentary and economic independence for Ireland from Westminster. The Volunteers began to display their military muscle in support of the Patriot Party in Dublin and together they were soon successful in their demands. After Grattan's Parliament had been established in 1782, some members of the Volunteers began to advocate further reforms, including Catholic emancipation. This proved a step too far for many and the movement split apart. The radical rump continued both with its political demands and its public parades until it was disbanded in 1793, but by that time it had lost much of its power and influence.

Volunteering and parading were particularly popular in Ulster, where over 300 companies had been formed by 1782. Volunteer companies paraded on a range of Williamite and other royal anniversaries. They also marched to celebrate British military victories, to church services and to display their martial skills. From 1780 the movement also held general reviews, which incorporated mock battles involving thousands of volunteers, each summer in Belfast, Derry and elsewhere. The Volunteers used parades as part of their military training and to display the strength of the movement, but they also became popular social events which attracted large crowds of spectators out onto the streets. Newspaper reports suggested that the parades were particularly popular among women and girls, who came onto the streets to watch their menfolk parading in the brightly coloured uniforms, which were usually based on British Army designs. A scarlet jacket with a contrasting trim and trousers was the most popular design, but an increasingly diverse range of

Fig.14 The Lisburn and Lambeg Volunteers of 1782. Dunmurry, 1995.

styles was adopted. For a while parading became the most fashionable of activities, and for some, being seen in a uniform was more important than martial ability. A writer to the *Londonderry Journal* on 25 June 1779 reflected the cynicism that these developments had encouraged when describing the Volunteers as, 'Our cloud-cap't grenadiers and our gorgeous infantry . . . (who) after the amusement of a year . . . (are) satisfied with a fine coat and a firelock.'

However, most of the visual displays were more to do with political demands than with fashion. Each Volunteer company paraded with a distinctive flag, to identify it and distinguish it from other companies. Like the uniforms, these also drew on the wider military tradition: the flags bore the company name and its motto while in the centre was an appropriate image surrounded by a wreath of shamrocks or other floral emblems. A diverse range of subjects are found on the small number of surviving Volunteer flags. The most common design was the Irish coat of arms: a harp, usually with its forepillar in a female form and topped by the royal crown. Alongside this emblem of loyalty one might also see Hibernia, or Erin, wearing a toga and seated with one arm resting on a harp while holding a pike topped with a liberty cap in the other. Other flags emphasised loyalty to the Glorious Revolution, whose ideals the Patriots claimed had yet to be extended to Ireland. The flag of the Ballymena Volunteers carries a representation of two clasped hands with the cipher of King William III, while the Killeavy Volunteers from County Armagh bore a portrait of King William with the mottoes *Our King and Country* and *William's Great Cause*. Another prominent image, which is found on the flags of both the First Armagh Volunteers and the County Sligo Light Horse, depicted the sun bursting through clouds.

This variety of images indicates something of the diverse range of influences on, and ideals of, the Volunteer movement. They also indicate the pivotal role of the Volunteers for future political and social movements in Ireland. While the references to King William and use of the crowned harp indicate the wider loyalty to the monarchy, this is balanced by the importance of emblems of Ireland, and in particular the prominence of Hibernia. Feminised representations of Ireland were common in Gaelic tradition, but here Hibernia was used more specifically as a counterpoint to the figure of Britannia. Bearing a pike and a liberty cap, Hibernia was also identified with the continental, and French, radical tradition. These allusions were also enhanced by the use of the sunburst emblem on some banners, which was also a Masonic

Fig.15 The classic portrayal of King William III based on a painting by Jan Wyck appears on the banner of Dyan LOL No 1. Dungannon, 1993.

symbol of knowledge and enlightenment. Collectively, the Volunteer banners varied between professions of loyalty to the crown and symbols which resonate with demands for political reform. The banners were therefore being used as a more complex medium of expression, one that could indicate both group identity and political ideology. But the Volunteer movement could not resolve the tensions between the demand for radical political reform and loyalty to the crown and the movement fell apart. As it fragmented the dispersed membership variously joined the United Irishmen, the Orange Order and the militia. The parades of the early 1780s were the last time that Hibernia and King William would be incorporated within a common political ideal. They would soon come to

Fig. 16 In the late eighteenth century both Hibernia (or the Maid of Erin) and King William appeared on banners carried at parades by Volunteer companies. This unusual banner belonging to the Cookstown branch of the INF depicts Hibernia surrounded by other prominent Irish symbols such as the wolfhound, Celtic Cross and round tower. Lurgan, 1992.

. . . the Great Standard, elevated on a triumphal car, drawn by four horses with two volunteers as supporters, containing on one side of the canvas a representation of 'the Releasement of the Prisoners from the Bastille' motto *Sacred to Liberty*. The reverse contained a figure of Hibernia, one hand and foot in shackles, a volunteer presenting to her a figure of Liberty, motto *for a people to be FREE, it is sufficient that they WILL IT*.

symbolise the two polarised and conflicting traditions in Ireland.

As sectarian clashes became more serious in rural Ulster, the final Volunteer parades, held in Belfast on Bastille day in 1791 and 1792, continued to assert the internationalist ideals of political change. In 1791 the companies carried portraits of Benjamin Franklin and the Compte de Mirabeau alongside slogans denouncing the slave trade. The following year 800 Volunteers marched to the Falls review grounds, in Belfast, with the flags of the 'five free nations': Ireland, America, France, Poland and Great Britain; and they displayed:

The Volunteers left an enormous legacy for Irish social and political life even though they have not had the enduring impact of their political descendants: the United Irishmen and the Orange Order. The Volunteers drew on the existing customs of the guilds, the Freemasons and Williamite clubs and they elaborated and formalised parading as the most appropriate medium for public commemoration and celebration. They consolidated and extended the use of parades as a medium for binding together and expressing complex political, religious, cultural and social ideals, and as part of this process they expanded and elaborated the use of music and visual displays, until the performance became a central attraction of these events. In their essence the parades were shows of force and Grattan's Parliament was achieved through a blend of political argument, rhetoric and a thinly veiled military threat. When the movement broke into its conservative and radical wings, it had a significant influence on the growing sectarian divisions in Ulster and both the emergent Orange and Green traditions rapidly adopted parading as the appropriate medium for contesting, claiming and marking symbolic control of territory.

6

FREEMASONRY IN ULSTER

The Freemasons were another important element in the popularisation of parading in the late eighteenth century. The Grand Lodge of Ireland had been in existence in Dublin since at least 1725 when the first masonic parade was recorded through the city. However, Freemasonry only became a significant presence in Ulster in the 1780s and it underwent a second, and more extensive expansion between 1810 and 1830. In both periods the growth was especially dramatic in Counties Antrim, Armagh and Tyrone, an area that seems to have been particularly responsive to fraternal organisations. Always a secretive organisation, the role of Freemasonry in Irish history has not been addressed in any depth, but it is clear that Freemasonry was a broad church. It had its roots in the continental enlightenment tradition but it also adapted to local circumstances.

The description of the church parade of members of the Orange and Old True Blue lodges in Belfast on St John's day, 24 June 1781, records that the procession was headed by 'the Mayor and Corporation amounting to about 80 gentlemen preceded by a fine Band of Musick'. Two years later the worshipful master of the Orange Lodge, assisted by lodge members and other dignitaries, laid the first stone at the new White Linen Hall in Belfast. Lodge members contributed £100 towards the new building. These details suggest that membership of the Masonic Order at this time was drawn from the social elite, similar to the Volunteers. However,

counterbalancing the urban respectable Masonry was a less formal and less disciplined 'hedge-masonry' in rural areas. Rural Freemasonry appealed to a wide range of individuals of all trades and classes and membership of lodges in the rural areas of Antrim, Armagh and Tyrone, was often extremely diverse ranging from gentlemen and farmers to weavers, carpenters and 'pastoralists'. At its most basic the lodge was a source of mutual aid and fellowship: in south Antrim in the 1820s Masonic lodges acted as libraries, took out subscriptions to journals and provided facilities for self education as well as offering membership of a social network. But membership could also give access to a more extensive network of connections through social and political patronage. The Volunteers and the United Irishmen drew on this broad membership, while many of the founders of the Orange Order were also Freemasons and they drew freely on the structure and symbolism for their new body.

The St John's day parades, to honour their patron saint, were the most significant public events for the Freemasons and this was an important anniversary in Ulster. Some of the Belfast gatherings drew more than 30 lodges and some lodges are reported to have walked from as far as Comber to attend a parade in Belfast. However, it was more common for a lodge to parade to a local church service and numerous small gatherings were recorded each year in the local press through

'Notices of Thanks' sent to the local preacher. Lodges also paraded in all their finery at the funeral of a deceased member, and for many lodges such an event was almost an annual occurrence. The Freemasons always paraded in their regalia, the members wore aprons bearing a range of symbols while the officers often wore elaborately decorated cloaks. Each lodge also carried a banner, bearing its name, warrant number and many of the symbols of the brotherhood. Contemporary reports provide little information of the Masonic insignia that was displayed at parades but a number of early nineteenth century banners have been documented by historians of The Craft. These exhibit a wide range of sizes, colours and construction techniques (painted, embroidered, appliqué) but they all carry broadly the same image, the arch of brotherhood surrounded by the symbols of the institution. The key elements were the Royal Arch and the all-seeing eye, while surrounding the arch were a selection of symbols which were used in initiation through the degrees of the order and which, while they appear readily identifiable, have meanings specific to the brotherhood itself. Many of these symbols, such as the beehive, cockerel, three runged ladder, snake and ark of the covenant, were utilised by the early Orange Order and have subsequently been adopted by the Royal Black Institution. Although these often refer to identifiable biblical episodes their specific meaning is related to the rituals of the relevant body and, as Anthony Buckley has noted in his analysis of Black symbolism, such meaning remains private to the specific institution.

Until the mid nineteenth century, Freemasonry drew its membership widely from both Protestant and Catholic communities. However, membership of any single lodge was not necessarily mixed but rather tended to reflect the denominational make-up of the area. Masonic lodges could therefore be seen as either Protestant

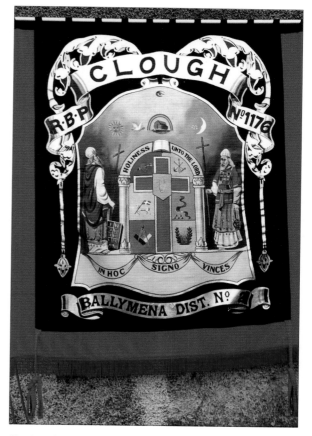

Fig.17 This collection of symbols relates both to biblical stories (Noah's Ark, Burning Bush and David's Sling) and also to levels of initiation within the Royal Black Institution. Many were taken directly from the regalia of the Freemasons as was the motto *In hoc signo vinces* (in this sign you conquer). Ballyclare, 1996.

or Catholic and as a result become embroiled in local sectarian rivalries. For example a Masonic parade on St John's day in 1828 was attacked at Galgorm on their way home from Ballymena, because the leader of the masons 'wore a white cloak ornamented with green crosses' and the group were considered to be Catholics and Ribbonmen. Several of the Freemasons were injured in the fighting before the authorities arrived. It is unclear whether there was any overlap with the regalia of Catholic groups such as the Ribbonmen because there are few contemporary descriptions and virtually no material remains, but in this case the Masons were seen as Catholics rather than as neutral. It seems clear that as sectarian clashes became increasingly common in south Ulster, it became ever more difficult for Freemasonry to bridge the sectarian divide. Masonic parades often became the target of attack, sometimes from Catholics and sometimes from Protestants, as the middle ground became increasingly narrow.

Freemasonry went into a decline as a popular organisation after the Party Processions Act, which prohibited all parades, was introduced in 1832. Until then the annual St John's day procession was a prominent event in the local Masonic calendar. Many lodges in Ulster had previously risked suspension from the Grand Lodge by ignoring internal bans on parades during the 1820s and 1830s, but the new legislation was more strictly enforced. After 1832 interest in the movement, particularly in rural areas, began to fade. In many areas the famine during the 1840s, with its destructive effects on rural communities, is claimed to have provided the final blow to popular non-sectarian Freemasonry. Although Freemasonry has continued to thrive in Ulster it has long been a predominately Protestant and middle class body and no longer holds public parades. Masonic parades were never as frequent, as large or as elaborate as the Volunteer parades, but the Freemasons played a significant role in helping to establish parading as a popular practice in Ireland. Furthermore they also had a powerful influence on the early Orange Order, many of whose members were themselves Freemasons, and they borrowed much from the organisational and symbolic displays of the masons when they established the new organisation.

EARLY ORANGE DISPLAYS

The Orange Order was formed in 1795 in County Armagh following clashes with members of the Roman Catholic Defenders outside Loughgall. The 'battle of the Diamond' was merely the latest in a series of sectarian disturbances that had occurred in the area since the mid 1780s. The formation of the Orange Order did nothing to quell these tensions, and their parades often erupted in violence. One man was killed at the first Orange parade in County Armagh in July 1796 and 14 people died at an affray involving Orangemen and the militia in Stewartstown, County Tyrone the following year. Violent clashes, with Ribbonmen, Freemasons and the authorities, occurred regularly through the early decades of the nineteenth century until all parades were eventually banned by the government under the 1832 Party Processions Act.

The Orange Order remained a predominately rural organisation until later in the century; it was strongest in the southern counties of Ulster and had only a small presence in Belfast. In the early decades its leadership was drawn from the rural gentry and the aristocracy but the mass of members was largely lower class. The order borrowed much of its structure and secrecy from the Freemasons, but its principal aims were to protect the Protestant interest and to perpetuate the memory of the Williamite military victories. The commemoration of the Boyne was the highlight of the Orange calendar from the

Fig.18 Dan Winter's Cottage outside Loughgall where the Orange Order was formed after the battle of the Diamond in 1795 (see also Fig. 83). Dungannon, 1993.

foundation of the institution. A description of an early parade taken from a letter from Lord Gosford of Markethill to Lord Camden, the lord lieutenant, in Dublin, dated 13 July 1796, and reproduced in Crawford and Trainor (1969), shows the importance of visual displays to the order from its inception. Lord Gosford notes that 30 companies of Orangemen arrived at Markethill after parading through Portadown, Loughgall and Richhill and requested to march through his demesne. They arrived, he wrote:

> . . . about five o'clock in the evening marching in regular files by two and two with orange cockades, unarmed, and by companies which were distinguished by numbers upon their flags. The party had one drum and each company had a fife and two or three men in front with painted wands in their hands who acted as commander. The devices on the flags were chiefly portraits of King William with mottoes alluding to his establishment of the Protestant religion, and on the reverse side of some of them I perceived a portrait of his present Majesty with the crown placed before him, motto *God Save the King*.

The Twelfth parades quickly grew in significance across Ulster; they were held in an ever-wider variety of locations and were attended by large crowds. The anniversary was also marked by elaborate visual displays. Orange arches are well documented from 1812 onwards, and flags were flown from churches and other prominent buildings. Often the success of the event was determined as much by the numbers of flags or banners on display as by the numbers of people who paraded. The *Belfast News Letter* noted that in Lurgan in 1815 there were 120 'beautiful flags', at Hillsborough in 1828 there were more than 200 flags, and in 1848 the paper reported that, in Belfast on 13 July, ' . . . the banners were of the most costly fabric and the most elegant designs and as they floated in the morning breeze they

presented a spectacle of great beauty and splendour'.

While it appears that it was important for each lodge to identify itself with an elaborate flag or banner displaying the lodge name and warrant number, the range of images they carried was very limited. King William on his white horse at the Boyne seems to have appeared on most banners. The Orange Order programme for the Twelfth in 1980 cites a description by Dr John Gamble, who passed through Tandragee on the Twelfth in 1812, noting that there were, '. . . a number of orange banners and colours, more remarkable for loyalty than taste or variety, for King William on horseback, as grim as a Saracen on a signpost, was painted or wrought on all of them.'

The other images that were used did little except affirm a loyalty to faith and crown. The Hanoverian monarchs seem to have been well represented in the pre-Victorian era but otherwise only the 'Crown and Bible' was a readily identified subject. A report in the *Northern Whig* of 15 July 1845 refers to 'banners . . . covered with emblems more mysterious far than ever Masonic badge or symbol gave to view', and suggests that some Orange banners carried an array of initiation symbols similar to contemporary Black banners, but there is no other evidence for this until much more recently.

As with contemporary banners, the early displays largely ignored recent events and instead emphasised abstract ideals and continuity with the past. One exception to this, however, was a banner carried at Coleraine and described by *The Irishman* on 16 July 1824. It portrayed:

> . . . a man prostrate at the foot of His Majesty's horse, with the face towards the feet and the horse trampling on him . . . I was told that a person named Doey . . . was killed at the fair at Garvagh . . . about

11 years ago, by the Orangemen in a quarrel, and that it was to perpetuate the memory of the transaction they painted him in that way on that flag.

While flying party flags and erecting arches in prominent locations often seems to have been done partly to show the dominance of Protestants in any given area, banners were not normally used in this way. This seems to be a unique example of a banner being used directly and openly to taunt members of the Catholic community.

Flags and arches were still only erected as part of short-term displays: the arches were little more than bunches of orange, purple or blue flowers strung across the road and the flags seem to

have been made by local haberdashers in the days preceding the event. Both of these forms of display were put in position early on the morning of the Twelfth and only expected to last the day. The banners, on the other hand, were more substantial artefacts. Newspaper reports often commented on the quality or the costliness of the fabric that was used and on the skill involved in the embroidering of detailed images on either side. Sometimes gold thread or a mixture of fabrics was used in their manufacture and this was time-consuming and skilled work. The making of banners was not professionalised until much later in the century and these early embroidered or sewn banners were probably made and repaired by the wives, mothers and other relations of Orangemen, although local tradesmen were also called upon. As banner making became more industrialised in the late nineteenth century, painted images became the norm. However, a small number of banners and bannerettes are still sewn and embroidered today.

Fig.19 The Crown and Bible image is among the most longstanding of the Orange Order banners. The reference to the interconnection between faith and monarchy is similar to the RBI 'Red Cross and Crown' banner. Note also the all-seeing eye which appears widely on Black banners in particular (see Figs 8 and 17). Saintfield, 1993.

Fig. 20 A small number of embroidered banners can still be seen at parades. This one from Blackscull, Co Down includes a wide range of Black symbols and depicts many of the biblical stories that are important to the organisation. Scarva, 1993.

R I B B O N M E N

Catholics began to organise to defend their community and parade to celebrate their history and culture under the name of Ribbonmen from about 1810. The Ribbonmen were the inheritors of the tradition of Defenders (who joined with the United Irishmen in 1798), but they remain a shadowy organisation. The name was used by groups across Ulster but little is known of their structure or organisation, although it is assumed from the few recorded oaths that they too drew on the Masonic traditions. They seem to have drawn membership from a broad range of rural Catholic society with the leadership being supplied by the more educated traders and farmers.

In the early nineteenth century St Patrick's day was widely celebrated in a leisurely manner by 'drowning the shamrock'. As had once been the custom for the Williamite anniversaries people gathered together to eat and to toast their history and culture. St Patrick's day parades are less widely recorded but it is clear that by the 1820s groups of Ribbonmen had begun to hold parades on 17 March in a number of locations. *The Irishman* of 22 March 1822 noted that Catholics in County Down had agreed not to hold their annual procession because of violent clashes with Orangemen the previous year, even though it was an 'immemorial practice' and 20,000 'men and women dressed in their beloved green' had been involved in the march. The paper also asked 'should not the Orangemen do likewise?' Because of the often-inclement weather in March, opposition to Catholics parading in many towns and villages and recurrent tit-for-tat violence, these parades never grew as large as their Orange counterparts.

The evidence of Ribbonmen regalia or artefacts is very poor. There is little documentation apart from a single drawing of a Ribbon collar dating from 1840. Newspaper reports from the 1820s suggest that Ribbonmen identified themselves by wearing white or green ribbons on their hats and either 'white handkerchiefs about their waists' or a sash. While green is widely recognised as the main colour used by Irish nationalists, white also has a long tradition of use among the Catholic community, particularly in rural areas. It was the colour of the Houghers in Connaght in the 1710s, the Jacobites in the 1720s, the Whiteboys in the 1760s and the Defenders in the 1790s. The Ribbonmen, therefore, symbolically linked themselves to a deep-rooted tradition.

Ribbonmen regularly carried flags and colours but again there is little information about these. A report in the *Northern Whig* of a parade in Crossgar in March 1849 readily dismisses them: 'there were twelve flags – pitiful, paltry rags'. More details are offered by the *Northern Whig* in its report of 20 March 1847 of a parade in Seaforde where the Ribbonmen were 'accompanied by the usual paraphernalia, viz, fifes, drums, sashes and flags inscribed with mottoes and devices; also several having the portrait of St Patrick'. From this meagre

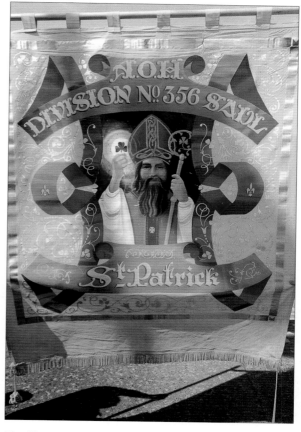

Fig. 21 The most common portrayal of St Patrick depicts him in his robes of office casting the snakes out of Ireland. Note also the round tower, Celtic Cross and Rising Sun that appear widely on both AOH and INF banners. Toome, 1995.

Fig. 22 A more recent version of St Patrick which abandons many of the traditional symbols and has adopted a modern design for the banner. Derry, 1995.

information one could speculate that the Ribbonmen parades would have looked broadly similar in form to those of the Orange Order and the Freemasons. All three groups carried flags and banners with emblems, symbols and insignia of their respective organisation, members wore sashes and other devices in distinctive colours, and all three marched to the sound of fifes and drums.

RESPECTABLE PARADING

Early nineteenth-century parades were largely lower class events, albeit with some support and patronage from sections of the gentry. The authorities regarded them as troublesome, if not dangerous, events which were to be tolerated where necessary and controlled wherever possible. The Party Processions Act was briefly allowed to lapse in the late 1840s but further sectarian clashes, culminating in the 'battle' of Dolly's Brae outside Rathfriland in 1849 led to its re-implementation. The law was largely successful in restraining popular processions, if not support for them. Orange opposition to the anti-parading legislation was led by William Johnston of Ballykilbeg, whose campaign of civil disobedience in the late 1860s led to his imprisonment, but this in turn provided his platform to win a Westminster seat in Belfast in the 1868 general election. Parades began to be organised in a regular manner from 1870 onwards although the law was not repealed until 1872.

The mobilisation of Protestant opposition to the Party Processions Act was one of two key events that marked a turning point in the culture of parading. The other was the electoral reforms of the 1880s which extended the franchise and increased the political importance of the working classes. Beginning in the 1870s but more significantly from the 1880s, parades were supported and utilised by the political leadership of the emergent nationalist and unionist movements, especially once the campaign for Home Rule dominated the political

Fig. 23 William Johnston of Ballykilbeg who campaigned against the prohibitions on parades in the 1860s and insisted that the right to parade should extend equally to Catholics and Protestants. Saintfield, 1993.

agenda. The annual cycle of parades became important political events and an opportunity to display political and national allegiances. Politicians began to use the parades to build support, to mix with the voters and to work their constituency. The meeting at the field, once largely restricted to religious matters, was now increasingly used as a political platform. The heightened political tensions meant that violence still flared at and after parades. This was now a less widespread occurrence than in the earlier years of the century, but remained problematic in growing urban areas such as Lurgan, Portadown and Derry and particularly in Belfast where the Orange Order grew rapidly in power and significance after 1870. Urban sectarian riots punctuated the final decades of the century.

The Williamite anniversaries, which had long been acknowledged as expressions of popular loyalty to the crown, became more widely supported by the middle classes and the political elite and participation was encouraged as an expression of a Protestant-Ulster-British identity. This Ulster Unionist identity slowly emerged as the earlier Protestant acceptance of their Irishness was compromised in the face of a growing radicalisation of Irish nationalism which emphasised its Catholic and Gaelic heart and demanded Home Rule if not independence. While some intellectuals continued to emphasise the plurality of Irishness, popular sentiment became increasingly polarised. St Patrick's day, which had long been the most popular of Irish Catholic public celebrations, was eclipsed by the anniversary of the Feast of the Assumption or Our Lady's day on 15 August. This was adopted for nationalist celebrations from 1872 and from the 1880s parades became a prominent feature of the Home Rule campaign and processions were regularly held in towns and villages with a large Catholic presence across Ulster. The emergent marching season was thereby consolidated as both a popular and a respectable fact of life in the north of Ireland during this period.

In the changing political climate, in which parades took on a greater prominence, the banners

Fig. 24 The Virgin Mary. Downpatrick, 1992.

that were carried by the individual lodges took on more significance. Unfortunately very little regalia, or detailed descriptions of regalia, survive from before the end of the nineteenth century. Those that have survived exhibit a wider range of sizes and styles than modern banners. Most lodges carried regalia that was made at home rather than professionally, and the decoration, done with embroidery or appliqué rather than by painting, employed female skills rather than male. The size and style of the regalia also varied enormously from banner to banner and reflected this varied manufacture. Some lodges carried flags, others carried banners comparable to present day examples. Some flags, such as the one reputedly carried by Rathfriland Orangemen at Dolly's Brae in 1849, and now in the Orange Museum in

Loughgall, were similar in size and style to military flags, made of plain white cloth with a simple appliqué design featuring a square and compass within an arch. Others were similar in design to modern banners, the one belonging to Sandy Row Heroes seen in a photograph dating from about 1868 (in the House of Orange in Belfast) had a central square image depicting *The Secret of England's Greatness* surrounded by a border 18 inches wide. Few, however, will have matched the banner that the Cookstown True Blues carried through the town in 1874 and which according to the *Belfast News Letter* was 'borne by ten men (and) attracted universal attention'.

From the middle of the century new techniques of production and more standardised formats began to be adopted by professional banner painters. These innovations were devised in London by George Tutill, who developed a process of painting on silk, which was strong and remained flexible; more elaborate images could be produced and the banners lasted longer. Tutill's style of banner, in which a distinctive image was painted on a large rectangle of silk finished with a contrasting border, remains the basis for contemporary banners and many of the images his firm designed are still used for modern banners. These new banners were first produced for the growing trade union movement in England but the styles and techniques were soon adopted by Irish banner painters. Some of the Biblical images were easily transferred from a trade union aesthetic into Irish politics. Adam and Eve, Abraham and Isaac and the Good Samaritan, all of whom appear on Orange or Black banners, were once used as examples of trade union ideals. But local painters also devised their own images appropriate to the Irish context. Prior to the 1870s the range of images

was limited: the same few heroes and symbols appeared on the majority of the banners. They offered only simple messages of faith, loyalty and identity. All this began to change as the parades became more explicit displays of national identity. The banners began to be used to elaborate in more detail on the meaning of Irish nationalism and Ulster unionism, to expand the pantheon of heroes beyond King William and St Patrick and to emphasise both national ideals and local distinctiveness and difference.

Fig. 25 The story of the Good Samaritan has been widely used by fraternal organisations to represent their ideals. Ballyclare, 1996.

IMAGING IRISH NATIONALISM

The Orange Order remained the most prominent parading body within the Protestant community, but nationalist parades were organised by a diverse range of groups. Two of the most prominent of these were the Ancient Order of Hibernians and the Irish National Foresters. Both groups developed as a blend of political organisation and self help movement; they were part of the wider Irish nationalist community and drew on the wider British tradition of friendly societies, which provided a range of medical and funeral insurance for their members.

The Hibernians trace their roots back to sixteenth-century leader Rory og O'More although in practical terms they were heirs to the traditions and practices of groups such as the Ribbonmen, the Defenders and rural bands organised to protect the interests of the Catholic community. They grew increasingly powerful as a mass movement in Ulster politics in the early twentieth century when, under the leadership of Joe Devlin, they were closely allied to the Nationalist Party and established themselves as a Catholic counterpart to the Orange Order. The Irish National Foresters were formed as a result of a schism from the British-based Ancient Order of Foresters in 1877 in a dispute over whether the organisation should continue to participate in parades. The Irish members who wanted to retain their parading traditions formed a new

Fig. 26 The AOH claim their descent from Rory og O'More, a leader of the 1641 Rebellion against English rule in Ireland. O'More holds a banner with the Hibernian motto *For Faith and Fatherland* (see Fig. 6). Draperstown, 1993.

organisation and continued to participate in marches. In the late nineteenth and early twentieth centuries the AOH and INF along with other bodies such as the Land League, the United Irish League and the Gaelic League were

Fig. 27 Joe Devlin MP for West Belfast, who reorganised and revitalised the AOH in the early years of the twentieth century. Derry, 1993.

Fig. 28 The INF is a friendly society whose original aim was to provide assistance and insurance for members who fell ill or suffered ill fortune. Friendly societies were widespread in the nineteenth century. Many of them created elaborate costumes and regalia for their members as can be seen in this painting. Belfast, 1997.

prominent in extending the customs of parading within the nationalist community and developing the visual displays in support of Home Rule.

As the Catholic anniversaries became more openly political so too did the visual displays. At the first Lady day parade to Hannahstown, outside Belfast, in August 1872, the banners and flags were restricted to tried and trusted mottoes such as *Remember Limerick*, *God Save Ireland*, *Erin Go Bragh* (Ireland for ever) and depictions of the crownless Irish harp. In Derry, the banners portrayed popular icons such as St Patrick, Pope Pius IX and Daniel O'Connell. But within a few years a much wider range of political heroes were being portrayed. William Orr and Robert Emmet, political heroes

from the United Irishmen era, were carried alongside slogans demanding Home Rule at Downpatrick in 1874, while nationalists at Lurgan also portrayed Emmet, alongside Theobald Wolfe Tone and the Manchester Martyrs (three Fenians whose public execution in Manchester in November 1867 aroused anger and demonstrations throughout Ireland).

By the 1880s, contemporary politicians were also being widely portrayed on banners. At a parade and rally in Monaghan in 1884, portraits of Michael Davitt (founder of the Land League), TM

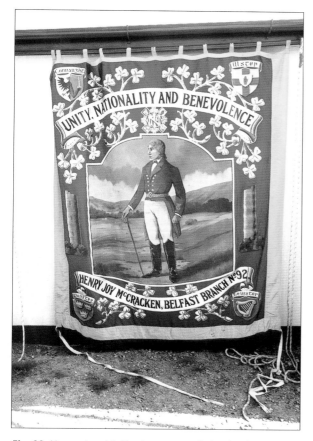

Fig. 29 Henry Joy McCracken, one of the leaders of the United Irishmen who was executed in Belfast in July 1798. Ballyholland, 1995.

Fig. 30 William Orr was a Protestant member of the United Irishmen from near Antrim who was executed in October 1797 for administering unlawful oaths. Lurgan, 1992.

Healy and Charles Stewart Parnell, appeared with the slogans *Land for the People* and *Ireland for the Irish*. Alongside these leaders of modern nationalism there were numerous references to the earlier generations of historical and religious figures. Daniel O'Connell seems to have been pre-eminent among the recent leaders, with Patrick Sarsfield, leader of James II's armies in 1691, Rory og O'More and Hugh O'Neill, two of the last great Gaelic chiefs representing earlier generations. Among the religious figures, St Patrick remained pre-eminent, but St Columbcille and the Pope were both widely depicted. Alongside these key personalities a range of established symbols and slogans continued to occupy a prominent place.

Hibernia with her harp; the crownless harp; the wolfhound and the round tower were all popular, as were the slogans *Erin go Bragh*, *Faith of our Fathers* and *God Save Ireland*.

As well as becoming openly politicised, the banners linked the campaign for Home Rule with the earlier rebellions and resistance to the British presence. Although the Home Rule movement was largely peaceful, the banners acknowledged the violent traditions of previous attempts for political independence and left the implication that the violence of the risings of 1798, 1803 and 1867 may be needed once more. The banners also linked the aspirations for a future free from British domination with a celebration of the Gaelic and

Fig. 31 Robert Emmet, who led an attempted rebellion in 1803 and was subsequently hanged in Dublin. Draperstown, 1993.

Fig. 32 St Columbcille (or St Columba) was an Irish saint who established the early Christian church in Derry. In the corners are portraits of Joe Devlin, John Redmond, John Dillon and TP O'Connor who were leading figures in the Nationalist Party during the Home Rule era. Draperstown, 1993.

Catholic past that was presented as a continuous and unbroken chain. St Patrick and the Pope were carried side by side with contemporary politicians and the Gaelic chiefs appeared as ancestors to the United Irishmen and the Fenians. The implications of the images on the banners were that all of these heroes of Ireland's past had gone to their deaths fighting for a Catholic nation, and the present generation were taking up their uncompleted tasks and were prepared to make the same sacrifices.

REDEFINING THE UNION

There are occasional reports which indicate that a wider range of images began to appear at Orange parades during the 1870s and 1880s. Banners depicting 'Brother Johnston of Ballykilbeg' had been seen at Banbridge in 1876 and by 1888 those carried by Belfast Orangemen 'bore the portraits of the friends of Protestantism and the leaders of the Conservative Party'. These included a diverse range of local preachers and politicians and national figures, among them Henry Cooke and Thomas Drew, Sir Edward Saunderson, Lord Salisbury and Lord Randolph Churchill. However, the depictions of King William and of the longstanding symbols of loyalty to Crown and Bible continued to dominate the visual displays.

Around the turn of the century the local press began to carry more detailed descriptions of the subjects that were appearing on the new, professionally produced, banners. The *Belfast News Letter* noted the following at the Twelfth parade in Belfast in its edition of 13 July 1901:

Fig. 33 The Rev Henry Cooke was a leading conservative Presbyterian preacher who was born in Maghera in 1788. He was prominent in arousing sectarian antagonisms in Belfast in the nineteenth century. Londonderry, 1995.

Several of the banners bore excellent portraits of King Edward VII, six banners had portraits of the late Queen, while 4 or 5 portrayed the late Dr Cooke. Those which did not depict scenes of 1690 or bear an emblem of the Bible and Crown, were devoted to portraiture. These included the Late Lord Farnham, Sir James Haslett MP, Sir James Henderson DL and Col Wallace (who is at present out in South Africa with his regiment). (The list continues with the names and titles of a number of minor personalities who were depicted on the banners.)

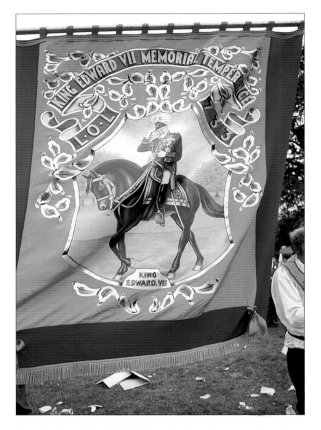

Fig. 34 King Edward VII. Monarchs have been portrayed on Orange banners since the earliest parades in 1796. Besides Edward VII, Queen Victoria and King George VI are also portrayed on contemporary banners and Queen Elizabeth II appears on a Scottish Orange banner. Belfast, 1995.

The correspondent of the *Northern Whig*, on 13 July 1901, noted the significance of the changes:

> The obverse of the banner in most cases retains the old time custom of immortalising the name and features of some champion of Protestantism, living or dead, local or national. But the half dozen designs that used to be the beginning and end of the reverse of the banners are no longer recognised as limiting selection and hundreds of Biblical and historical episodes are open to the banner painter now to choose from.

Although the writer may well have been exaggerating the variety of new subjects there clearly was a major increase in the range of subjects appearing on banners. Between 1904 and 1914 the local press gave some considerable coverage to the new banners that appeared each year. The *Belfast Weekly News* carried reports and descriptions of 77 new banners that were formally unfurled across Ulster (a ceremony which appears to have been introduced at this time). The *Belfast News Letter* gave brief descriptions of some 49 new banners designed by the Belfast banner maker, William Bridgett, when they appeared for the first time at the Belfast parade. These two records give a useful cross section of the new images that were appearing at this critical time for unionism. Categorising these new banners into broad subject groups can help to draw out some of the changes that were taking place in unionist thinking and attitudes.

Representations of King William were still the largest category of images, while other images of the Williamite wars were the second most important category. Altogether over 54% of the new banner paintings featured King Billy and related images. However, this was the first time that a wider range of events related to the Williamite era was depicted on banners. These images focus on the battles at the Boyne and at Aughrim, and emphasise William's personal role in the campaign. But they also highlight his presence in Ulster: landing at Carrickfergus and travelling through Belfast and Hillsborough on his way to the battlefield. These developments occurred at the same time as the debate was taking place among unionists over the legality and morality of military opposition to Home Rule and which eventually resulted in the raising of the paramilitary Ulster Volunteer Force. The increased emphasis on the military side of William's character could therefore be seen to emphasise the need for physical resistance and to legitimise the mobilisation of opposition to Home Rule.

Fig. 35 Many incidents relating to King William and the Williamite wars appear on Orange banners. These include his arrival in England at Torbay. Rossnowlagh, 1993.

Fig. 36 His arrival in Ireland as he is greeted at Carrickfergus. Larne, 1995.

Fig. 37 His departure from Hillsborough Castle en route to the Boyne. Dungannon, 1993.

Fig. 38 Leading his troops into battle at the Boyne. This image is based on a painting by Benjamin West. Saintfield, 1993.

Fig. 39 Being wounded in the battle. Rossnowlagh, 1993.

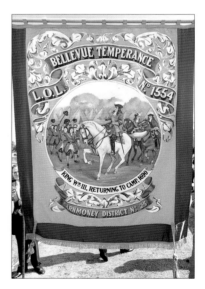

Fig. 40 Receiving the cheers of his soldiers as he returns to camp after the victory over James' army. Antrim, 1995.

The biblical and religious imagery, which began to appear at this time, can also be understood within the framework which legitimises the resistance to Home Rule. Religious symbols and Old Testament stories had been a central element of the iconography of the Freemasons since the eighteenth century and had been used by the Orange Order since its formation. Hitherto these had been publicly restricted to a few, abstract, coded expressions of the Protestant faith, but now they were made more elaborate and explicit. Historical figures such as Luther and Wycliff, Protestant martyrs like Latimer and Ridley, and Biblical characters such as Moses, Samuel, David and Goliath, Naomi and Ruth are represented for their metaphorical value, and as exemplars for the unionist plight. Assertions that the Ulster Protestants were God's Chosen People or even one of the lost tribes of Israel had existed since the seventeenth century, but it was only at this time that clear analogies were presented between the unionist position and that of the Israelites. It was at this crucial moment that biblical and religious history began to be used as a guide to practical action as much as for its moral teaching.

Long-established subjects such as the Crown and Bible, portraits of the monarch, declarations of faith and professions of loyalty remained popular, but the large number of banners depicting local subjects (politicians, dignitaries, buildings and places) was a new development. The representations were no longer simply abstract historical, religious and imperial ideals but increasingly an emphasis was placed on a local identity and local connections. Religious values were not simply expressed through imperial ideals and abstractions such as the Crown and Bible: they were now being localised. Abstract ideals were now embodied in the memory of radical Presbyterian preachers and grounded in the very bricks and mortar of neighbouring churches. The imperial

Fig. 41 Many of the Old Testament stories relate to the sufferings of the Israelites. Analogies have been made between the Ulster Protestants and the Israelites since at least the seventeenth century. Newtownbutler, 1994.

connection remained important and images of the monarch were still prominent on the banners, but from the turn of the century local religious leaders and politicians were feted with equal reverence.

Besides the historical and religious themes that dominated the visual displays there was also a more prosaic element which dealt with the pragmatic aspects of the relationship between Ulster and the Empire. The rapid industrial growth during the later nineteenth century had been a major factor in the growth of unionism. The Orange Order was not only about displays of faith and identity; it was also important in maintaining networks of political and economic patronage. Many lodges were linked with specific places or

Fig. 42 Many banners portray prominent local landowners, aristocrats, businessmen and politicians such as this example of the Earl of Erne and his ancestral home. Note also the demand for *No Dublin Interference* hung from the top of the banner. Belfast, 1996.

Fig. 43 Many other banners bear the portraits of local churchmen or former members of the lodge who would be unknown outside their immediate locality. Lurgan, 1993.

Fig. 44 Banners depicting prominent landmarks such as a church or the local Orange hall are also widely found. Rossnowlagh, 1993.

Fig. 45 It is less common to find other local references such as this painting of a sailing ship on the Islandmagee banner. Larne, 1995.

Fig. 46 In the past many lodges had been linked to specific trades or work places but bannerettes such as this one from the Naval Lodge are now much less common. Belfast, 1993.

Fig. 47 The banner of Crystal Springs LOL incorporates a blend of traditional symbols (Crown and Bible) with a celebration of more modern transport technology. Belfast, 1996.

types of work as well as the more common church or village based bodies. Images of trade and industry, the railways or the newspapers began to appear alongside local churches and stately homes. As a further part of the chain of patronage relationships, local businessmen, dignitaries and minor political figures were represented on the banners from this time.

In the extended period of heightened political debate over the long-term constitutional status of Ireland, the banners of the Orange Order were an important part of the public and political discourse of unionism. Depicting a wide range of contemporary local heroes, they drew clear connections between the historical past and current concerns, and stressed the importance of being ready and willing to take action rather than simply verbalising complaints. In all these instances the changes emphasise the emerging identity that is more clearly grounded in a sense of place, a community defined by its history of independence and a tradition located in Ulster. All these images help to confirm the centrality of the Order to the local social, political and economic environment. At the same time the banners were used to make clear visual connections between the more mundane aspects of social life and the emerging and developing sense of national identity which emphasised that the Protestant community in the north of Ireland were British rather than Irish.

The Orange Order consolidated and clarified its position in the years preceding the First World War, but it was not entirely without opposition from within the Protestant community. The Independent Orange Order (IOO) was set up 1902 by Thomas Sloan. It initially drew support from two areas, Belfast and North Antrim, where members of the urban working class and rural tenant farmers, respectively, disagreed with the leadership and policy of the larger body. The order

flourished for a few years as a radical voice within the Protestant community but gradually lost its urban support and it had lost much of its significance by the start of the First World War. However, the IOO retained a small rural base, largely in County Antrim, and consolidated itself as a voice of more fundamentalist Presbyterianism.

The Independent Orange Order remains a small organisation, although it has experienced a slight increase in membership in recent years. It holds an annual parade on the Twelfth which is often attended by the Rev Ian Paisley, although he is not a member of the institution. Their banners are similar in form and subject matter to those of the Orange Order. The events of the Williamite era and Biblical images are the dominant themes. But the banners give a greater prominence to the early leaders of the Protestant faith such as John Calvin and Martin Luther and some of them incorporate the rhetoric of 'born again' evangelical Christianity within their designs.

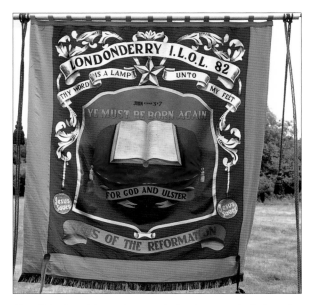

Fig. 48 Independent Orange Order banner depicting the open Bible, without a Crown, and the mottoes *Ye Must Be Born Again* and *For God and Ulster*. Portglenone, 1995.

Fig. 49 *(opposite)* Independent Orange Order banner portraying Martin Luther. Portglenone, 1995.

DEVELOPMENTS UNDER STORMONT

Most of the banners that can be seen at Orange and Green parades today are closely based on the designs that first appeared during later stages of the Home Rule campaign. The range of images has continued to expand with the inclusion of banners depicting local people and places, but only two major events have been incorporated into the broad corpus of Irish nationalism or Ulster unionism since the Home Rule era: the Easter Rising and the battle of the Somme. The Somme has been given a prominent position within Orange iconography, but the Easter Rising has less importance on nationalist banners. There are a number of reasons for this. Both the Hibernians and the Irish National Foresters lost much of their social significance in the immediate post war years. Lloyd George's introduction of a National Insurance scheme in 1911 undermined the importance of friendly societies throughout Great Britain and Ireland. Furthermore, as supporters of constitutional nationalism, the Ancient Order of Hibernians declined as a political force with the rise of Sinn Féin after the end of the First World War. Finally both organisations lost significance following partition as a result of the marginalisation of nationalist political groupings in the north and the legal and political restraints imposed on their public displays. Nevertheless both the AOH and the INF have maintained their annual parades and a small number of new images have subsequently

Fig. 50 A distinctive INF banner portraying Patrick Pearse. Ballyholland, 1995.

appeared on their banners. A number acknowledge the significance of 1916 for Irish nationalism. Portraits of Roger Casement and Patrick Pearse can be seen on INF banners and even the Hibernians make reference to the Rising, although only on a single banner in which James Connolly and other leaders surround an image depicting Daniel

Fig. 51 Daniel O'Connell handing a document entitled Catholic Emancipation to Hibernia. In the corners are James Connolly, Patrick Pearse, Thomas MacDonagh and Tom Clarke, four of the leaders of the 1916 Rising. The banner also includes portraits of two earlier figures, Thomas Emmet and Neil McGurk. Downpatrick, 1992.

O'Connell handing Hibernia a document entitled *Catholic Emancipation.*

Other developments on nationalist banners are difficult to trace. The local press has never had the same interest in nationalist parades as they had in Orange parades and the subjects of the banners were rarely described. The rise of republicanism and partition in 1921 removed most of the power and influence of the parading bodies such as the AOH and INF, which was tied up with the Irish Parliamentary Party. Under Stormont, it was increasingly difficult to hold nationalist parades in the north: if they were not banned outright they were constrained to strongly nationalist towns or

areas. As well as the larger organisations like the AOH and INF, some GAA clubs participated in the parading tradition by joining in at the major commemorations. GAA banners were prominent at the parades held in 1953 to commemorate the one hundred and fiftieth anniversaries of Robert Emmet and Thomas Russell and also at the parade along the Falls Road to mark the fiftieth anniversary of the Easter Rising, in 1966. They also joined a range of other nationalist groups at St Patrick's day parades in Belfast in 1971 and 1978 but do not seem to have appeared since them. The regalia of the republican movement was, until recently, dominated by the tricolour although they have begun to carry more formalised banners (see below). The AOH and the INF have continued to carry their banners on St Patrick's day, at Easter and in August although contemporary parades are still dominated by the subjects that could be seen during the Home Rule campaign: St Patrick, Hibernia and the heroes of the nationalist struggle.

In contrast to the marginalisation of the Hibernians and Foresters, the Orange Order was at the heart of the political order established with the creation of Northern Ireland. Consequently the events of 1912–16 appear as second only to the Williamite era on their banners. Subjects include Sir Edward Carson, the signing of the Covenant, the gunrunning ship the *Clyde Valley*, depictions of the battle of the Somme and portraits of various individuals who had been killed in the war.

The first banner commemorating the battle of the Somme, belonging to Hydepark LOL, was unfurled at Belfast in 1919 and images of the Somme were widely utilised on arches and murals through the 1920s and 1930s. However, representations of contemporary individuals were not introduced into the Orange canon so quickly because of restrictions that had been placed on the portrayal of the living. Until 1905 it was common practice to represent living politicians and other

Fig. 52 The attack of the Ulster Division at the Somme on 1 July 1916. The banner, which includes the Williamite motto *In Glorious Memory*, is based on a painting by J Prinsep Beadle. Larne, 1995.

Fig. 53 Sir Edward Carson, leader of the Ulster Unionists in their opposition to Home Rule. Lisburn, 1995.

Fig. 54 The *Clyde Valley* was used to smuggle in arms from Germany for use by the UVF in 1914. Lurgan, 1994.

public figures on Orange banners. This seems to have been little more than an extension of the elaborate system of political and economic patronage woven around Orangeism. In some cases the individual portrayed would graciously agree to ceremonially unfurl the new banner himself before it was taken off to the Twelfth parade. The decision to change the rules came about after William Pirrie, a partner at Harland and Wolff, who was portrayed on at least one Orange banner, expressed less than unambiguous support for the Union. Although he was not a nationalist, his liberal political views brought him into conflict with the Orange Order and clearly made him an unsuitable figure to be honoured at parades. In order to prevent any similar future embarrassments, the Grand Lodge ruled that henceforth no living persons should be honoured in such a way. This ruling seems to have been resisted for a few years, but by the 1920s it was generally accepted. Sir Henry Wilson was the first of the leading Unionist opponents of Home Rule to appear on a banner when his portrait was displayed

at the Belfast Twelfth in 1926, four years after he was killed in London by members of the IRA. Other figures and events were only slowly incorporated into the larger body of images. When Bridgett Brothers published a catalogue of their main Orange and Black banner designs in 1930, they were dominated by the traditional Williamite and religious themes; only *The Battle of the Somme* depicted a recent event. Since this time, a broad range of new images has appeared, although the majority are found on only one or two banners. Many of these serve to commemorate victims of IRA violence or depict local war memorials. Others pay tribute to organisations such as the B Specials or the UDR which have special significance for many Protestants and which have been disbanded in recent years. One final small category of images depicts symbols which relate to the formation of Northern Ireland or the status of Ulster within the United Kingdom and in many ways functions as modernised representations of the Crown and Bible motif which has been used for so long.

Fig. 55 This banner commemorates two members of the Ulster Special Constabulary killed by the IRA in Rosslea in 1921 during a period of intense conflict immediately prior to partition. Newtownbutler, 1994.

Fig. 56 Another rare reference to early twentieth century violence, the banner commemorates the killing of six Protestants at Altnaveigh in June 1922. Rossnowlagh, 1993.

Fig. 57 A bannerette commemorating the Ulster Special Constabulary. Belfast, 1995.

Fig. 58 Memorials to the war dead are another common feature of Orange banners. Lurgan, 1993.

Fig. 59 Many banners make references to the union with Great Britain but this one belonging to the Elizabethan Temperance lodge includes a quotation from Queen Elizabeth II which states *I shall always strive to repay your loyalty* and dated July 1953. Lurgan, 1993.

Fig. 60 The Bleary Crimson Star banner provides a biblical background for the British presence in Ireland. Lurgan 1993.

LOCAL CHANGES

The broad developments and changes that I have been describing took place slowly and over many decades. There are a number of factors which account for the slow rate of change. Banners are expensive and can often last a generation or more, in some cases perhaps only a few new banners appear each year; furthermore each of the institutions is conservative and some considerable emphasis is placed on maintaining local customs and practices. Nevertheless the changes did take place and it can be interesting to consider how and when the broad changes in style, form and design were implemented across the north. Accurate data on the effects that standardisation and professionalisation had on local lodges is not widely available from the generally published information. It is largely restricted to the minute books of individual lodges and such records are fragmentary. Information on variations in the use of particular images is also somewhat haphazard. However, in recent years several district and county Orange lodges have published histories of their areas for anniversaries such as the tercentenary of the Boyne, the bicentenary of the Order or for other local occasions. Among the areas that are covered are Ballynafeigh, the Clogher Valley, Fermanagh, Larne, Omagh and Richhill. Some indications of how the changes took place can be gleaned from these sources although the quality and detail of information on the banners varies considerably.

One such booklet entitled *An Historical Account of Orangeism in Lecale District No 2 Co Down*, was published in 1990 for the Tercentenary of the battle of the Boyne. It was compiled from the minute books of 21 lodges in the area, some of which had been in continuous existence since 1798. This provides some details of the changes and developments of the banners of a group of geographically connected lodges over an extended period of time.

The earliest references to visual displays are to flags. Hollymount LOL 1465 records carrying Orange flags 'as early as 1840', Killyleagh True Blues LOL 549 spent £1 2s 9d on materials to make a flag in 1867 and £2 7s 1d to make another in 1870. In 1884 they bought a flag from a Mr N Dane of Belfast which seems to have lasted until 1925 when £34 of the profits of a bazaar were spent on a new banner. Further banners were unfurled in 1950 and 1978. The JA McConnell Memorial, Downpatrick LOL 431 unfurled a new flag in July 1896, which was described as 'a copy of flags carried by the Army of the time':

> It was 3' by 3'6" in size, made of blue silk, with a small Union Flag in one corner and a gold bullion fringe . . . it was sent to the firm of Mr Thomas Stevens, in Coventry, to be embroidered with a wreath of Orange Lilies, enclosing the figures '431',

with a scroll, top and bottom, with the words 'Downpatrick Orange Lodge'.

Other flags of this period seem to be more like contemporary banners in style. Ballygawley LOL 1898 bought a flag in 1892 for £6, with a portrait of King William on one side and *The Secret of England's Greatness* on the other. Woodgrange LOL 1073 purchased a flag in 1895 for £3 12s 6d, this was blue with an orange fringe and depicted King William crossing the Boyne on one side and a Crown and Bible on the reverse. The district lodge bought its first banner in 1891, but none of the individual lodges record buying banners before the turn of the century. Ballygawley bought one in 1901, Woodgrange in 1903 and Ballyclander LOL 1563 in 1905. John Irvine Memorial, Ballydonnell LOL 1446 laid their flag to rest in 1902 when it was used to cover the coffin of William Johnston, district master for 45 years and one of the most notable Orange figures of the nineteenth century. The flags

Fig. 62 The painting entitled *The Secret of England's Greatness* depicting Queen Victoria handing a Bible to an Indian prince has been used on Orange banners since the high point of the British Empire. Lurgan, 1993.

Fig. 61 Flags were once the dominant visual display at parades but this photograph illustrates the difficulty of seeing the images they might bear. Belfast, 1993.

of many lodges lasted much longer: Cumberland True Blues of Crossgar LOL 358 only bought their first banner in 1924; Inch LOL 430 and Ballykilbeg LOL 1040 not until 1932.

Most of these lodges seem to have bought three or four banners over the course of this century. Ballygawley, the first in the area to buy a banner, unfurled new banners in 1901, 1917, 1952 and 1975. Woodgrange had new banners in 1903, 1938 and 1968; Killyleagh True Blues in 1909, 1934, 1950 and 1978; Rathmullen LOL 360 in 1930, 1968 and 1985; and Toye Purple Banner LOL 1077 in 1921, 1934 and 1972. Some of these seem to have lasted little more than 12 years but for many 25 to 30 years was not uncommon. The banner bought by Ballyculter in 1911 from Bridgett's for £20 6s was not replaced until 1953, while that bought by Killyleagh True Blues in 1925 was later 'presented to a newly formed Lodge, LOL 1688, which met in the House of Commons', when the lodge unfurled their new one in 1950.

The images they carried were typical Orange designs. Nineteenth-century regalia was dominated by portraits of King Billy but with the commercialisation of banner production, more subjects came to be featured and most lodges opted to change at least one design when they replaced the banner. Although this brought some changes it was more of a rotation than an increase in the range of images. Lodges often simply chose to replace one monarch or local hero with another. The Ballygawley flag depicting *The Secret of England's Greatness* was followed by one portraying Queen Victoria in 1917, King George VI in 1952, and with *My Faith looks up to thee* in 1975 but all bore a painting of King William III on the other side. Woodgrange had a Crown and Bible on their last flag, the first banner in 1903 depicted Queen Victoria, the next in 1938 Lord Carson and the current one Hollymount Parish Church. Killyleagh True Blues' new banner in 1950 had portraits of William Johnston and the Rev McCleery while the replacement depicted the relief of Derry and the Ballyculter lodge replaced Wycliffe and the First English Bible with a depiction of Jesus in 1985 while maintaining the King William on the other side. King William clearly remained the dominant image throughout the century but others seem to have been changed depending on the interests or fancy of the current members and banners were

regularly used to honour recently deceased lodge members. A similar range of images can be seen at present day Orange parades; the details may have changed but not the overall style. Most of the lodges do not record where they purchased their banners but the name of Bridgett Brothers occurs frequently and this indicates the importance of the banner painter in creating a degree of continuity in the corpus of images and maintaining the traditions that they helped to create.

Fig. 63 The majority of biblical references are drawn from the Old Testament, however depictions of Jesus appear on a small number of Orange banners. Dungannon, 1993.

THE BLACK, THE APPRENTICE BOYS, THE JUNIORS AND THE WOMEN

Under Stormont the loyal orders flourished. The Twelfth of July became a ritual of state in all but name, and most senior political leaders were members of the Orange Order or another marching order. However, it was only in the 1920s and 1930s that the loyal orders consolidated their position and extended their parades and displays more widely across the north. The Black parades on the last Saturday in August and the Apprentice Boys and Junior Orange parades at Easter all date from this time. As well as the Orange Order there are a number of other closely linked loyal orders which organise parades and contribute to the variety of visual displays. The Royal Black Institution is the senior branch of Orangeism. It is regarded as more religious in its orientation and its members tend to be more elderly and conservative. All members of the Black Preceptories are also members of the Orange Order, but not all members of the Orange Order are also in the Black. Black lodges were first recorded in the the late eighteenth century although the institution only began to have a public impact in the early part of the twentieth century when members began to parade at Scarva for the Sham Fight on 13 July.

The Apprentice Boys of Derry is the oldest of the loyal orders. The first club was formed in 1714 to commemorate the 13 apprentice boys who were responsible for closing the gates of Derry to James' approaching forces. However, the organisation was only brought together as a single body in 1859. There are eight Apprentice Boys parent clubs based in Londonderry, each of which has a number of branch clubs both in Ireland and elsewhere. Junior Orange lodges first appeared in the 1880s, they became more formalised in the 1930s only to decline after the Second World War. They have recently experienced a revival of interest. Similarly interest in the Association of Loyal Orangewomen has fluctuated since its earliest appearance in the middle of last century and as with the juniors there has recently been something of a resurgence of interest.

The *Belfast Weekly News* of 20 July 1824 reported on the prominence of Black parades in Scotland, and asked, 'Why don't the Black Preceptories in Belfast have an annual demonstration of their own? They are sufficiently strong enough to have a very respectable turnout'. Until that time the only Black parade seems to have been held in Dungannon to commemorate the Siege of Derry, although elsewhere Blackmen attended Orange parades. Black parades only really became prominent after the First World War when the organisation took over the existing parade and Sham Fight at Scarva (which had been recorded since the 1830s). However, it was only in the 1920s that the Last Saturday in August became established as their major parading day and marked the formal close of the marching season. Black banners were occasionally recorded at Orange

Fig. 64 Many Old Testament stories illustrate God's protection of the faithful, or they may illustrate how God will provide an answer for those who truly believe. Prominent among the banner images are those of Noah, on the ark. Scarva, 1993.

Fig. 65 Moses and the Burning Bush. Newtownbutler, 1994.

Fig. 66 Elijah fed by Ravens, Ballyclare, 1996.

Fig. 67 Daniel in the lion's den, Scarva, 1993.

Fig. 68 David slaying Goliath under the maxim *He that would be free must strike the first blow*. Scarva, 1993.

Fig. 69 Similar examples are occasionally drawn from the New Testament, such as the story of the Wise Men following the Star. Portadown, 1993.

parades in the decade prior to the First World War but they only seem to have begun to be widely seen in the inter-war years. As nowadays, their banners were dominated by symbols of the institution and illustrations of biblical stories.

As Anthony Buckley has clearly demonstrated, these banner illustrations are neither a random sample of popular biblical stories nor are they taken evenly from all sections of the Bible. Instead the images draw heavily on the Old Testament and focus on themes which emphasise the trials and tribulations of the Israelites and on their unwavering faith in their status as God's Chosen People. Depictions of Noah on the ark, Moses by the burning bush, Moses leading his people across the parting Red Sea, Daniel in the lions' den, David slaying Goliath and Gideon and his Three Hundred are all demonstrations of the power of God to fulfil his promise to his people. Similarly the few New Testament stories that appear, such as the Three Wise Men, also emphasise the need to maintain faith against the odds. Black banners have few references to history or the Williamite wars but rather, prefer to make a simple and clear analogy between the position and plight of the Ulster Protestants and with the Israelites of Biblical times.

In contrast to the relatively recent development of Black parades, the Apprentice Boys parades, held each August and December in Derry, can be traced back to the eighteenth century. Nevertheless, it was not until the early twentieth century, and the construction of an extensive railway network, that they attracted members from further afield. The August event in particular thrived in the years after the Second World War when newspaper reports suggested that it grew in scale virtually every year. It was only at this time that the Apprentice Boys began to carry banners like the Orange Order. Until this time they normally carried either flags or bannerettes.

However, the problem with flags was that unless it was windy it was difficult to see the images. The *Belfast News Letter* of 15 August 1960 noted that a number of Apprentice Boys' clubs were carrying bannerettes to increase the visibility of the displays: 'There had been a tradition of flags only for Apprentice Boys parades, but these require a breeze for effective display. Some clubs have compromised by carrying bannerettes.' In recent years there has been a steady shift towards the standard banner format but even today flags and bannerettes are

Fig. 70 Apprentice Boys banners are more narrowly focused than either Orange or Black banners. The vast majority of images relate in some way to the siege of Derry. The Closing of the Gates in December 1688 by the 13 apprentice boys marked the beginning of resistance to the Jacobite forces. The siege in a formal sense began in April 1689 and was lifted in August that year when the *Mountjoy* broke through the boom across the Foyle to bring much needed supplies to the inhabitants. Banbridge, 1993.

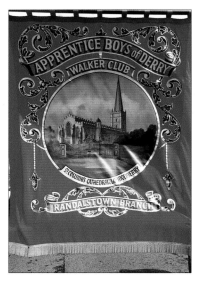

Fig. 71 The siege came to an end in August 1689 when the *Mountjoy* sailed up the Foyle estuary and broke the boom across the river. The Relief of Derry is warmly welcomed by the Rev Walker and other inhabitants. Ballymoney, 1995.

Fig. 72 Many Apprentice Boys branch clubs carry portraits of the leaders of the resistance. Londonderry, 1995.

Fig. 73 A small number depict prominent local landmarks such as St Columb's Cathedral. Londonderry, 1995.

still more common at Apprentice Boys parades than at other loyal order events and they dominate the December parade when the weather is often inclement. However, many clubs also have full size banners which they display at the August parade.

The Apprentice Boys have a much narrower range of images than either the Orange Order or the Royal Black Institution. The vast majority of their banner designs are related to the main events of the siege of Derry: *the Closing of the Gates*; defending the City Walls; *the Relief of Derry* and the *Mountjoy* breaking the boom across the Foyle. Others feature the leaders of the defence: the Rev George Walker, Major Henry Baker, Captain Browning, Colonel John Mitchelburne and Adam Murray all have clubs named after them and appear on bannerettes. Interestingly, Henry Campsie, who was one of the 13 Apprentice Boys, has a club named after him but his portrait does not appear on the banners. Other images depict

such important symbols as the coat of arms of the city, Roaring Meg (the cannon used in the defence of the city), St Columb's Cathedral or other prominent local buildings. As with the Black banners there are scarcely any references to other Williamite events or to more recent happenings. At their two main parades the focus is on the city of Derry which continues to be held up as the supreme exemplar of both the Ulster Protestant plight and as an indicator of the unwavering determination of the Protestant people to resist any changes.

There is also a range of banners and bannerettes at the small, but growing, number of Junior Orange parades and the limited number of Women's Orange parades. Junior Orange banners are normally smaller in size than those of adult lodges but take the same form and style. The images are related to the themes addressed by the senior body although they have a specific

Fig. 74 Junior Orange banner portraying the young Prince William. Larne, 1993.

Fig. 75 Junior Orange bannerette of Jesus the Good Shepherd. Carrickfergus, 1995.

Fig. 76 Women's Orange Lodge bannerette depicting the widely used image – *My Faith Looks Up to Thee* (see also Fig. 88). Rossnowlagh, 1993.

orientation towards young people. The parades are therefore still dominated by Williamite images but a number of banners depict William of Orange as a prince rather than as a king. Similarly many of the biblical illustrations also have a special relevance to children – an infant Samuel, or the young David or Jesus 'suffering the little children to come unto him'. In contrast the few women's bannerettes that appear in public merely replicate the images carried by the male lodges and offer no distinctive female perspective on the Ulster Protestant position.

15

PARALLEL PASTS, PARALLEL LIVES

Ulster unionism and Irish nationalism have in part defined themselves through the images on the banners, and as such have each laid claim to differing events in the past. The two bodies of images refrain from making any explicit reference to the other community and much historical knowledge is implicitly assumed rather than relentlessly hammered home. By ignoring the presence and the experiences of the other community they can more easily focus on the consistency of their own sufferings and their particular sense of destiny. It is perhaps stating the obvious to say that each community uses the banners to present its own perspective on the past; however, if the various groups of images are brought together, we would see that in many cases they both acknowledge the importance of the same event, although for very different reasons. And when one untangles the variety of images that are on display, one can see that both sides focus on the same few dates and experiences, which they regard as defining the parameters of Irish history. Themes of oppression and resistance, mistrust and betrayal, martyrdom and sacrifice are ones that drive the communities onwards and at the same time keep them apart. Such themes underpin not just the military histories of the two communities, but provide the rationale behind the inclusion of a number of the other subjects, such as the diverse religious, social and political heroes represented at the displays.

Both sides acknowledge the special significance of the seventeenth century and place considerable emphasis on the 1640s and the Williamite period. Nationalist banners celebrate the campaign led by Owen Roe O'Neill, and the battles of Curlew Pass and Benburb, while Orange banners commemorate the massacre of Protestants at Portadown in 1641 and the eventual defeat of the rebels following the arrival in Ireland of Oliver Cromwell. Each of the loyal orders commemorates various aspects of the Williamite campaigns between 1688 and 1691 and, as noted above, recall many of the principal events and characters of that era. Nationalists celebrate little from this time although they do commemorate Patrick Sarsfield, leader of the Jacobite forces during the successful defence of Limerick. The two military leaders appear on the banners as a virtual mirror image, both holding their swords aloft to inspire their armies. William sits on his white steed with red, white and blue livery, Sarsfield on his bay horse dressed in green, white and gold. The banner portraits are therefore not so much faithful representations of particular individuals but rather, a condensation of symbolic meanings which incorporate both national and moral characteristics.

Both nationalist and unionist groups carry banners related to the late eighteenth century, a period which marks both the beginning of the modern cycle of rebellions against English rule in

Fig. 77 The events of the Irish rebellion of the 1640s are remembered on both Orange and Green banners. The Orange Order commemorate the slaughter of Protestants at the River Bann in 1641 on this banner belonging to a Portadown lodge. Portadown, 1993.

Fig. 78 Hibernians, on the other hand, commemorate the 1640s through the figures of Rory og O'More (Fig. 26) and the military leader Owen Roe O'Neill, who led the Irish forces at the battle of Curlew Pass in 1645. Derry 1995.

Fig. 79 Owen Roe O'Neill's army also won a victory over Monro's army at the battle of Benburb in the following year, 1646. Downpatrick, 1992.

Fig. 80 The rebellion was finally crushed by Oliver Cromwell, who raised the seige of Drogheda with much bloodshed in 1649. The reverse image on this banner portrays Oliver Cromwell with the motto *Trust in God, but keep your powder dry.* East Belfast, 1993.

Fig. 81 Much is made of the importance of King William's white horse, but it was a common symbolic device to depict a military leader in such a way and in such a heroic pose. Note how William's colours are restricted to red, white, blue and orange. Saintfield, 1993.

Fig. 82 Patrick Sarsfield, leader of the Irish armies in the defence of Limerick in 1691, is depicted in a comparable pose to King Billy while dressed in green, white and orange. Derry, 1995.

Fig. 83 The battle of the Diamond in 1795 precipitated the formation of the Orange Order. Note the central figure on the white horse. Loughgall, 1995.

Fig. 84 The battle of Antrim, one of the key events in the United Irishmen rising in the north in 1798, is depicted using similar artistic conventions. Ballyholland, 1995.

Fig. 85 Many fraternal organisations were linked to the temperance movement in some way and a number of Orange lodges retain the word in their name (see Figs 88 and 89). Father Mathew was a prominent temperance campaigner in the early nineteenth century. Ballyholland, 1995.

Fig. 86 John Mitchel, leader of the failed uprising of 1848. Lurgan, 1992.

Fig. 87 Benjamin Disraeli, Earl of Beaconsfield, leader of the Conservatives and opponent of Gladstone's attempts to introduce Home Rule in the 1880s. Portadown, 1993.

Ireland and the consolidation of sectarian difference in the north. The Orange Order does make an acknowledgement of the Volunteer movement, but otherwise focuses on events that are linked to its own formation such as the battle of the Diamond in 1795 and Dan Winter's Cottage. Nationalist images concentrate on the events and personalities of the United Irishmen era, depicting the battle of Antrim in 1798 and such key figures in Irish nationalist historiography as Henry Joy McCracken and Robert Emmet. In contrast the events of the nineteenth century are poorly served on the banners. Greater prominence is given to constitutional politicians and religious leaders such as Daniel O'Connell, the temperance campaigner Father Mathew, or Benjamin Disraeli and the Rev Henry Cooke than to actual events, although John Mitchell (leader of the failed rebellion of 1848) is commemorated on the banner of the Newry branch of the INF.

I have already discussed the importance of 1916 for both communities. The Easter Rising is acknowledged as an important event in nationalist history but for both the Hibernians and the Foresters it appears as one of a chain of events, and its leaders are given no great preference over other nationalist leaders. In a similar fashion the Orange Order has incorporated the battle of the Somme into their wider iconography and several banners bear portraits of individuals killed in the First World War but the core of Orange sentiment remains rooted in the seventeenth century.

Both groups of banners are dominated by military and political history, with their focus on heroic victories, noble sacrifices and gallant leaders. But the corpus is wider than military history and a diversity of religious events, icons and symbols are interwoven among the battles and heroes. These broader bodies of work also address more personal elements which make the broad abstractions of nationalism and unionism more immediate and relevant to individual members and bystanders. A

large number of banners emphasise the importance of religious faith for the two communities, so one finds images of the Virgin Mary, St Patrick and the Pope in the same parade as Patrick Sarsfield and Daniel O'Connell while elsewhere Moses and Jesus might appear alongside King Billy and Edward Carson. There are also other more generalised notions of faith: the Orange banner which depicts a woman hanging onto a cross in stormy sea accompanied by the slogan *My Faith looks up to Thee*; or the image of Queen Victoria handing a bible to an Indian prince with the motto *The Secret of England's Greatness*. Yet more personalise the importance of religious belief so that concepts of sacrifice and martyrdom can be read through political and religious idioms. Orange banners show Hugh Latimer and Nicholas Ridley, Bishops of Worcester and London respectively, being burned at the stake in Oxford in 1555, and Margaret Wilson, who was drowned in the Solway Firth in 1685 rather than renounce her faith. Both Hibernian and Foresters banners use the example of Oliver Plunkett, Bishop of Armagh, who was hung, drawn and quartered in London in 1681. However, alongside these figures of historical and national importance, there is still room for lesser mortals, and many banners honour the sacrifices that have been made by local people for their country. This may take the form of commemorations of individuals who have been killed in recent wars or during the Troubles, portraits of local politicians, churchmen or other dignitaries who might have been linked to the lodge. This continues the custom that began at the end of last century when the patronage of local gentry, clergy or employers was an important factor in the social prominence of many of these bodies. Some of these depictions therefore hold up local people as exemplars, others appear in deference to the social system.

Another aspect that is broadly similar on both unionist and nationalist banners relates to

Fig. 88 The image of a woman hanging onto a cross in stormy sea, entitled *My Faith looks up thee* has been used by the loyal orders since the end of last century and appears widely on Orange, Black, Junior and Women's banners (Fig. 76). Bangor, 1994.

Fig. 89 The image of the burning of Bishops Latimer and Ridley in 1555 often includes either the slogan *Suffer unto death rather than submit to Popery* or Bishop Latimer's final words *Be of Good comfort Brother Ridley and play the man, we shall this day light such a candle by God's grace in England as I trust shall never be put out.* Belfast, 1995.

Fig. 90 The Catholic martyr St Oliver Plunkett is one of the rare figures who appears on both Hibernian and Foresters banners. The corner portraits depict Irish church leaders. Maghera, 1993.

Fig. 91 Margaret Wilson was tied to a stake in the Solway Firth and drowned by the rising tide for refusing to give up her faith. Portglenone, 1995.

depictions of women. Among the pantheon of dead male role models carried by the living sons of Ulster and Ireland one finds occasional female figures. But in contrast to the assertiveness of the male warrior or defender of his people, women have a much less active role. Scarcely any real women appear on banners: only idealised or symbolic representations of the female form are depicted. For example, both traditions utilise female symbols to represent their nation, a practice dating from the late eighteenth century when it was widely used among emerging western democracies. Britannia and Hibernia are used to personify their respective countries. Britannia appears dynamic, assertive and expansive with a lion at her feet and with her navy in the background. Hibernia, on the other hand, is often seen in a more passive mode, seated and surrounded by a mixture of cultural and natural

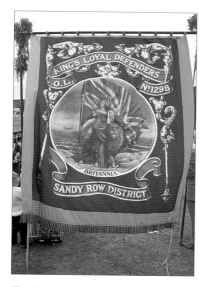

Fig. 92 Britannia is depicted in a heroic and militaristic pose with the lion at her side and a battleship in the background. Belfast, 1992.

Fig. 93 Hibernia, in contrast, is surrounded by cultural and historical symbols while the sun rises on a new day. Ballyholland, 1992.

Fig. 94 St Brigid is one of the few female figures to appear on the banners. Ballyholland, 1995.

artefacts: the harp, round tower, Celtic Cross and wolfhound. On the horizon a new day is dawning and perhaps offers the possibility that this will be the time when 'Her day will Come'. But feminised images depict a limited range of roles for woman. She is idealised as a mother/nurturer figure through Mary, or as an asexual saint in the form of Brigid, or is portrayed as the temptress Eve who led Adam to be expelled from the Garden of Eden. In contrast to the active hero, the ideal woman is portrayed as a passive figure. She clings to the cross, awaiting her salvation rather than actively seeking it as the male heroes do. She devotes herself to her faith to the point that she is willing to die for it. Apart from biblical characters and Queen Victoria, Margaret Wilson is the only female portrayed on any of the banners but she hardly represents an ideal role model. The images are conservative; they reflect both the symbolic values and the actual roles allotted to, and expected of, individuals in society in Northern Ireland. But they also help to reinforce them. Alongside the well-known celebrations of male military prowess and leadership, these images of women are equally important reminders of what Ulster and Ireland expects from its womenfolk.

16

TRADE UNION BANNERS

Trade unions or combinations were nominally illegal in Ireland between 1729 and 1824, but numerous associations were in existence throughout the eighteenth century, and as already noted (p15), these bodies often paraded on their patron's day or in displays of loyalty to the crown. The unions did not establish their own annual parading calendar in Ireland during the nineteenth century, but rather their main displays of strength were as part of major nationalist demonstrations. They came out in strength in support of Daniel O'Connell in 1830 and later attended his Repeal mobilisations. At the centenary of his birth in 1875 some 58 unions joined in the procession through Dublin. Trade unions also commemorated the Manchester Martyrs and supported Home Rule and Land League demonstrations from the 1870s onwards and held occasional May day parades during the 1890s and the early twentieth century in Belfast, Dublin and Newry. The close identification of unions with nationalism throughout Ireland reduced their growth in the north and restricted the unions from creating a distinctive parading tradition. However, following partition, May day parades, organised by the Belfast Trades Council, became an established event in the trade unions' calendar and although the parades have remained small affairs, the banners are still brought out each year.

Nineteenth-century banners displayed a mixture of trade union symbols and patriotic, nationalist images. St Patrick, Daniel O'Connell and Hibernia were widely depicted during the 1860s and 1870s and were later joined by figures as diverse as Brian Boru, Robert Emmet and the leaders of 1798. Although nationalist heroes and symbols were always prominent on trade union banners, they were far from the only subject matter. Some banners carried depictions of saints or biblical figures who could be identified with various trades: St Crispin appeared as patron saint of shoemakers, and Adam and Eve were depicted on the Belfast Tailors Union banner. It is interesting to note that the representation of Adam and Eve used on this banner remains the standard image of the biblical couple and can be seen on contemporary Orange and Black banners. A number of banners focused on the type of work the union members undertook. Sometimes this was displayed among the paraphernalia of heraldry – as in the example of the Drogheda Brick and Stonelayers Union – in other cases the banners portrayed men and women in the act of work. Two fine examples of this style are the banners of the Boyne Fishermen and the Drogheda Labourers Society, which are among a number of early banners on display in Drogheda Museum. In both of these cases the workers are overseen from the corners by nationalist icons, St Brigid and St Patrick in the first case, and Daniel O'Connell and Wolfe Tone in the second.

Fig. 95 James Connolly was a prominent trade unionist before his involvement in the Easter Rising in 1916. Belfast, 1993.

Few contemporary trade union banners retain references to nationalist heroes and ideals. The Belfast branch of the Irish Transport and General Workers Union has retained the portraits of James Connolly (who worked for the union in the years before the Rising) and James Hope (a prominent local member of the United Irishmen) on either side of its banner for most of this century. These two images were retained even after the union changed its name to the Services, Industrial, Professional and Technical Union in 1990. The Belfast Trades Council banner has a flag of each of the four provinces of Ireland in each corner with the council name in both English and Irish and the slogan 'Workers of the World Unite', while Derry Trades Council also have a bilingual banner. Others reflect the general aspirations of trade unions without narrowing them to a specific political ideology. *Peace, Work, Progress* appears on banners of the Amalgamated Transport and General Workers Union (ATGWU) and National

Fig. 96 One side of the Belfast Trades Council banner focuses on the local economy. Belfast, 1993.

Fig. 97 The other side is bilingual and reflects the internationalist perspectives of the trades union movement. Belfast, 1993.

Fig. 98 This ATGWU banner makes political demands rather than carrying representations of specific trades. Note the clasped hands similar to those used by the Hibernians (Fig. 13). Belfast, 1995.

Communications Union, *A Better Life Together* appears on the banner of the Northern Ireland Public Service Association (NIPSA).

Most trade union banners are dominated by the symbol or emblems of the union or they display some reference to the work or trades the union represents. The Post Office Workers banner has the union emblem on one side while the other image illustrates the diversity of work within the Post Office and the Union of Construction and Allied Trades and Technicians (UCATT) Northern Ireland banner depicts the construction industry, a joiner's shop and shipbuilding. Most of the banners belonging to branches of the Amalgamated Transport and General Workers Union reflect its size and diversity by depicting a broad range of work from shipbuilding to textile trades.

Sometimes these images reflect the changes that have been taking place in working practices in recent decades, as in the case of the Carter's Branch of the ATGWU, which depicts both a drayman with his horse and cart and a modern lorry. But an increasing number of unions reflect these changes in a more abstract way by adopting new and very different styles and designs for their banners. Many of the banners that have been made for new or amalgamated trade unions are much smaller in size than the standard banners; the imagery is more dramatic or 'modern' in its style. These banners also make little use of the traditional forms of design and no longer include heraldic emblems and floral motifs; in this they perhaps reflect something of the changes in the contemporary industrial world.

Fig. 99 Many trade union banners, such as this example from the Graphical, Paper and Media Union, have incorporated new designs into the traditional format. Belfast, 1995.

Fig. 100 The banner of the Carters' branch of the ATGWU reflects its history through the portrayal of both traditional and modern modes of transport. Belfast, 1995.

Fig. 101 Some newer unions have abandoned traditional forms and designs as in this example from the Communication Workers Union. Belfast, 1995.

Fig. 102 The Manufacturing, Science and Finance Union has also adopted a modern design. Belfast, 1995.

17

BAND BANNERETTES AND REPUBLICAN BANNERS

Two recent developments in visual displays have been a product of the Troubles – bannerettes carried by loyalist marching bands and banners carried by republican groups. Both categories of displays are relatively small in total but both are also increasing in number and in range of designs.

Music has always been a feature of the parades but many of the newer bands have remained independent of the loyal orders and are often critical of their conservatism although they are vocal supporters of the right to parade. These blood and thunder bands have become a major feature of the urban parades adding considerably to the noise and colour of the events. Many of the bands are led by a colour party who often carry an array of flags as well as an individual band bannerette. These often have little more than coats of arms, heraldic devices or representations of the Ulster, Scottish or Union flags on them but some carry the insignia of the Ulster Volunteer Force or of contemporary paramilitary groups while a few commemorate band members who have recently died. Although paramilitary regalia is nominally banned from Orange parades, the bands have introduced a range of references to the UVF, the Ulster Defence Association and the Red Hand Commando. Young Citizen Volunteers and UVF regalia are the most common and most, if not all, such bannerettes and flags include the battle honours from the First World War. This aims to

legitimise these displays as a means of honouring the groups who opposed Home Rule. However, it is impossible to claim historical allegiance for either the UDA or the Red Hand Commando regalia and such displays are much less common than the UVF displays. Each of the main paramilitary groupings has a degree of support within the loyalist communities; they each display their presence on

Fig.103 Many loyalist band bannerettes draw on symbols and designs that are used by the loyal orders. Bangor, 1993.

Fig.104 Others emphasise the Protestant military tradition ranging from the siege of Derry and the Boyne to the battle of the Somme and the B Specials. Londonderry, 1995.

Fig.105 Many include the regalia of the original Ulster Volunteer Force and Young Citizen Volunteers in their designs. Belfast, 1994.

Fig.106 Others include symbols used by contemporary paramilitary groups. Belfast, 1996.

murals in the working class areas of Belfast and elsewhere and it would be surprising if similar displays did not appear on the parades as well.

In parallel with these developments an increasing number of groups within the republican movement have begun to carry more traditionally styled banners at commemorative parades. During the early days of the Troubles, republican demonstrations often ended in rioting or disturbances, but over the years a number of major anniversaries, for Internment, Bloody Sunday, and the Hunger Strikes, as well as many local commemorations, have become established as occasions for parades with more elaborate visual displays of support. Many of the banners remain simple affairs, slogans or group names painted on plain cloth and carried by hand, but in recent years some groups and some republican bands have taken to carrying more elaborate banners closer to the traditional style. Many of these newer banners commemorate a particular republican figure or an IRA volunteer who has been killed in the Troubles.

Their centrally-positioned portrait is often surrounded by republican symbols; others simply display symbols, such as the phoenix, with appropriate slogans or demands. In most cases these banners carry an image on one side only.

Fig.107 Republican banners draw widely on contemporary iconography as in this painting depicting an IRA funeral salute. Derry, 1997.

Fig.108 Republican banners are often linked to specific political campaigns such as this one for *Saoirse* ('freedom'). Belfast, 1996.

Fig.109 Many commemorate members of the IRA who have been killed in recent years such as this banner bearing a portrait and quotation from Mairead Farrell who was killed by the SAS in Gibraltar. Belfast, 1996.

Fig.110 The 1981 Hunger Strikers also feature widely on Republican banners such as this one belonging to the Kevin Lynch Flute Band. Derry, 1997.

18

RECENT DEVELOPMENTS

The displays that are being made on loyalist band bannerettes and republican banners; the development of new styles and designs on trade unions banners; and the small number of banners carried by independent preachers and missions that join some loyal order events all show the continued importance of making striking visual images at parades. Such practices were even maintained during periods of imprisonment by members of paramilitary groups, for example both UVF and UDA prisoners organised flute bands and held commemorative parades while in the Long Kesh / Maze Prison.

In contrast, the subjects portrayed by the unionist and the nationalist marching orders appear to have remained relatively static since the early part of the century. However, new images and new subjects do continue to appear on loyal order

Fig.111 Bannerette used by UDA prisoners. Londonderry, 1998.

Fig.112 Banner carried by members of the Old Forge Gospel Mission ahead of the Twelfth parade in Belfast in 1994.

Fig.113 Only a small number of banners portray victims of the recent Troubles. John Tennyson and Raymond Mayes were killed in a bomb attack on an Hibernian club in Lisburn in January 1976.

Fig.114 George Seawright, one time DUP councillor, killed by the IPLO in 1987, is remembered on the banner belonging to a Belfast branch of the Campsie Apprentice Boys Club. Lurgan, 1994.

banners. In recent years new banners have commemorated the demise of such locally significant bodies as the B Specials and the Ulster Defence Regiment. They have also served as memorials to individuals killed in the Troubles or as commemorations of prominent individuals such as John McMichael and George Seawright who had been members of one of the loyal orders. Banners have also honoured the victory of the allies in the Second World War, an event that has otherwise largely been ignored. Others display issues of more localised importance such as the banner depicting the Donaghadee lifeboat in action. References to contemporary events remain rare although one unusual example appeared on the banner of Lurgan Faith Defenders ILOL depicting the visit members of the lodge made to the Boyne Valley with their Lambeg drums. Nationalist groups have incorporated few new subjects in recent years: new

banners often reproduce the images of old ones. Two exceptions are the banner of the Lisburn Hibernian division portraying two local men killed in the Troubles and that of the Island Hill division depicting the visit of Pope John Paul II to Ireland in 1979, which shows him stepping out of the plane in front of the Aer Lingus logo.

Flags and banners have been an important feature of parades in Ireland since the earliest records and they continue to be a dynamic element at the events. These recent developments suggest that new images may continue to appear on banners as long as they are carried at parades. They illustrate how the banners continue to be used to elaborate on the history, heroes, ideals and aspirations of the major communities in Northern Ireland. They remain a valuable resource for those who wish to display their faith in their history, their traditions, their nation and their church.

Fig.115 A recent banner commemorating the victory of the Allies in the Second World War. Belfast, 1996.

Fig.116 A banner from a Donaghadee lodge depicting the local lifeboat. Rossnowlagh, 1993.

Fig.117 The banner of Lurgan Faith Defenders Independent Orange Lodge depicts them parading at the Boyne with their Lambeg drums. Portglenone, 1995.

Fig.118 The visit of Pope John Paul II to Ireland in 1979 is celebrated on the banner belonging to Island Hill Division. Draperstown, 1993.

ACKNOWLEDGEMENTS

The research on which this book is based was carried out between 1990 and 1998. The work has been carried out with the assistance of grants from the Economic and Social Research Council, the Cultural Traditions programme of the Community Relations Council and the Central Community Relations Unit. Publication of the book has also been supported by the Community Relations Council.

I would like to thank all those people who allowed me to photograph their banners at the numerous parades that I have visited over the years and especially those who found time to talk to me about their banners and answer my questions.

I would also like to thank Margaret McNulty and Catherine McColgan at the Institute of Irish Studies for their encouragement and patience in bringing this project to fruition.

The banner of the Belfast Unemployed Centre at the May Day parade. Belfast, 1995.

SOURCES AND BIBLIOGRAPHY

Until recently there have been relatively few publications dealing specifically with the history of parades and the associated visual displays in Ireland, although a number of academic articles have touched on aspects of this topic in passing. Several recent publications have attempted to redress this imbalance, these include a number of my own works dealing with the history of parading, contemporary parading culture and the use of visual displays. The following are a selection of those publications which deal specifically with parades or visual materials, each of them also has an extensive range of references which help link the culture of parading into a wider range of historical, political, sociological and anthropological studies:

Jarman, N (1997), *Material conflicts: parades and visual displays in Northern Ireland*, Oxford, Berg.

Jarman, N (1992), 'Troubled images: the iconography of loyalism' in *Critique of anthropology,* vol 12, no 2.

Jarman, N (1993), 'Intersecting Belfast' in Bender, B (ed), *Landscape: politics and perspectives*, Oxford, Berg.

Jarman, N (1998), 'Material of culture, fabric of identity' in Miller, D (ed), *Material cultures: why some things matter*, London, UCL Press.

Jarman, N (1999), 'Commemorating 1916, celebrating difference: parading and painting in Belfast' in Forty, A and Kuchler, S (eds), *The art of forgetting.* Oxford, Berg.

There are a number of other books and shorter articles, which deal with aspects of contemporary parading culture:

Bell, D (1990), *Acts of union: youth culture and sectarianism in Northern Ireland*, Basingstoke, Macmillan. Deals with Loyalist bands in Londonderry.

Bryan, D (forthcoming), *Orange parades: ritual, tradition and control*, London, Pluto Press. A study of the history and development of the Orange Order and their parades.

Bryan, D (1997), 'The right to march: the parading of loyalism in Northern Ireland' in *International journal on minority and group rights*, vol 4, no 3 / 4. Parades in Portadown and the current cycle of disputes.

Bryan, D (1998), 'Ireland's very own Jurassic Park: the mass media, Orange parades and the discourse on tradition' in Buckley, AD (ed), *Symbols in Northern Ireland*, Belfast, Institute of Irish Studies. An analysis of the media reporting of parades.

Bryan, D and Tonkin, E (1997), 'Political ritual: time and temporality' in Boholm, A (ed), *Political rituals*, Gothenburg, Institute for advanced studies in Social Anthropology. A comparative study of parades as political rituals.

Buckley, AD and Kenney, M (1995), *Negotiating identity: rhetoric, metaphor and social drama in Northern Ireland*, Washington, Smithsonian Institute Press. Includes pieces on Black banners, loyalist bands and violence at parades.

Cecil, R (1993), 'The marching season in Northern Ireland: An expression of a politico-religious identity' in MacDonald, S (ed), *Inside European identities: ethnography in Western Europe,* Oxford, Berg. A study of the Twelfth and Lady's day parades.

De Rosa, C (1998), 'Playing nationalism' in Buckley, AD (ed), *Symbols in Northern Ireland*, Belfast, Institute of Irish Studies. A study of nationalist parades and republican bands.

Fraser, TGF (ed, forthcoming), *We'll follow the drum: the Irish parading tradition*, Basingstoke, Macmillan. A collection of essays dealing with the broader history and culture of parading in Ireland, England and Scotland.

Larssen, SS (1982), 'The glorious twelfth: a ritual expression of collective identity' in Cohen, A (ed), *Belonging: identity and social organisation in British rural cultures*, Manchester, Manchester University Press. An analysis of the meaning of the Twelfth in rural Ulster.

Walker, B (1996), *Dancing to history's tune: history, myth and politics in Ireland*, Belfast, Institute of Irish Studies. Contains an essay on festivals and commemorations.

There are also three recent reports which deal with aspects of the current cycle of parade disputes but which also discuss the history of parades and the meaning they have for people in Northern Ireland:

Bryan, D, Fraser, TGF and Dunn, S (1995), *Political rituals: loyalist parades in Portadown*, Coleraine, Centre for the Study of Conflict, UUC.

Jarman, N and Bryan, D (1996), *Parade and protest: a discussion of parading disputes in Northern Ireland,*

Coleraine, Centre for the Study of Conflict, UUC.

Jarman, N and Bryan, D (1998), *From riots to rights: nationalist parades in the north of Ireland*, Coleraine, Centre for the Study of Conflict, UUC.

There are several works that deal specifically with aspects of the visual and symbolic culture linked to parades:

Bryson, L and McCartney, C (1994), *Clashing symbols: a report on the use of flags, anthems and other national symbols in Northern Ireland*, Belfast, Institute of Irish Studies. A wide-ranging analysis of a variety of contemporary visual and other symbols.

Buckley, AD (1985–6), 'The chosen few: biblical texts in the regalia of an Ulster secret society' in *Folk Life*, vol 24. An analysis of the symbolic content and metaphorical meanings of Royal Black Institution banners.

Buckley, AD and Anderson, K (1988), *Brotherhoods in Ireland*, Cultra, Ulster folk and transport museum. A brief illustrated survey of all the various brotherhoods and marching orders.

Gorman, J (1986), *Banner bright: an ilustrated history of trade union banners*, Buckhurst Hill, Scorpion. Deals with the development of banner making and specifically with trade union banners in England and Scotland.

Hayes-McCoy, GA (1979), *A history of Irish flags from earliest times*, Dublin, Academy Press. A heavily illustrated history of military, national, social and political flags and banners of all types.

Loftus, B (1978), *Marching workers*, Belfast, Arts Councils of Ireland. An exhibition catalogue of trade union regalia and artefacts containing an essay and many illustrations.

Loftus, B (1990), *Mirrors: William III and mother Ireland*, Dundrum, Picture Press.

Loftus, B (1994), *Mirrors: orange and green,* Dundrum, Picture Press. These two heavily illustrated studies deal with a range of visual and material artefacts that are used by the two dominant communities in Ireland.

O'Cuiv, B (1978), 'The wearing of the green' in *Studia Hibernica*, no 17 / 18. The historical development of nationalist symbols.

Sheehy, J (1980), *The rediscovery of Ireland's past*, London, Thames and Hudson. A study of Irish symbolism across a range of media.

The following are a selection of the main articles and books which have some references to parades or some relevance to their development and which situate the use of parades within the broader political context.

Firstly, some details of the very early history of parades in Britain and Ireland can be found in:

Rubin, M (1991), *Corpus Christi,* Cambridge, Cambridge University Press. This deals with the symbols and rituals surrounding this important festival.

Webb, J (1929), *The guilds of Dublin*, Dublin, Three Candles. Contains a description of the earliest Guild parade in Ireland among other things.

Seventeenth-century parades and commemorations, especially those relating to key events in the Protestant calendar, are discussed in their political and social context in the following:

Barnard, TC (1990), 'Crises of identity among Irish Protestants, 1641–1685, in *Past and present,* no 127, May 1990.

Barnard, TC (1991), 'The uses of 23 October 1641 and Irish Protestant celebrations' in *English historical review*, October 1991.

Hill, J (1984), 'National festivals, the state and "Protestant ascendancy" in Ireland, 1790–1829' in *Irish historical studies* XXIV no 93.

Kelly, J (1994), '"The glorious and immortal memory": commemoration and Protestant identity in Ireland 1660–1800' in *Proceedings of the Royal Irish Academy*, vol 94C.

Simms, JG (1974), 'Remembering 1690' in *Studies,* Autumn 1974.

A number of studies deal with the Jacobites, the Whiteboys, the Oakboys, the Volunteers, the Freemasons and other aspects of eighteenth-century society:

Barrington, J (1830), *Personal sketches of his own times*, vol 1, London, Coburn and Butley.

Bartlett, T (1992), *The fall and rise of the Protestant nation: the Catholic question 1690–1830*, Dublin, Gill and Macmillan.

Beames, M (1983), *Peasants and power: the Whiteboys movement and their control in pre-Famine Ireland*, Brighton, Harvester Press.

Crawford, WH and Trainor, B (eds, 1969), *Aspects of Irish social history*, Belfast, HMSO.

Connolly, SJ (1992), *Religion, law and power: the making of Protestant Ireland, 1660–1760*, Oxford, Clarendon Press.

Donnelly, J (1981), 'Hearts of oak, hearts of steel' in *Studia Hibernica*, no 21.

Joy, H and Bruce, W (1792–3), *Belfast politics or a collection of debates, resolutions and other proceedings of that town in the years 1792 and 1793*, Belfast, Joy and Company.

Kee, R (1989), *The most distressful country: the green flag* vol 1, Harmondsworth, Penguin.

Macrory, P (1988), *The siege of Derry*, Oxford, Oxford University Press.

Smyth, PDH (1979). 'The Volunteers and Parliament, 1779-84'. In Bartlett, T and Hayton, DW (eds). *Penal Era and Golden Age: Essays in Irish History 1690-1800*, Belfast, Ulster Historical Foundation.

Smyth, J (1993), 'Freemasonry and the United Irishmen' in Dickson, D, Keogh, D and Whelan, K (eds), *The United Irishmen, republicanism, radicalism and rebellion*, Dublin, Lilliput Press.

Stewart, ATQ (1993), *A deeper silence: the hidden roots of the United Irish movement*, London, Faber and Faber.

Discussion of parades and commemorations in the nineteenth century and of the early history of the Orange Order and the Ribbonmen can be found in the following:

Crawford, WH and Trainor, B (1969), *Aspects of Irish social history*, Belfast, HMSO.

Garvin, T (1981), *The evolution of Irish nationalist politics*, Dublin, Gill and Macmillan.

Garvin, T (1987), 'Defenders, Ribbonmen and others: underground political networks in pre-Famine Ireland' in Philpin, CHE (ed), *Nationalism and popular protest in Ireland*, Cambridge, Cambridge University Press.

Gibbon, P (1975), *The origins of Ulster unionism*, Manchester, Manchester University Press.

Kee, R (1989), *The bold Fenian men: the green flag*, vol 2, Harmondsworth, Penguin.

Kee, R (1989), *Ourselves alone: the green flag*, vol 3, Harmondsworth, Penguin.

O'Keefe, TJ (1990), 'Who fears to speak of '98: the rhetoric and rituals of the United Irishmen centennial, 1898' in *Eire-Ireland* XXVII:3.

Reid, T (1823), *Travels in Ireland*, London, Longmans.

Select committee (1835), *Report from the select committee, appointed to inquire into the nature, character, extent and tendency of Orange associations or societies in Ireland*, London, House of Commons.

Wright, F (1996), *Two lands on one soil: Ulster politics before home rule*, Dublin, Gill and Macmillan.

A number of local histories of Orange lodges have been produced in recent years by various county or district lodges. More focused consideration of the history of the Orange Order can be found in:

Dewar, MW, Brown, J and Long, SE (1969), *Orangeism: a new historical perspective*, Belfast, House of Orange.

Haddick-Flynn, K (1999), *Orangeism: the making of a tradition*, Dublin, Wolfhound Press.

McClelland, A (1990), *William Johnston of Ballykilbeg*, Lurgan, Ulster Society.

Senior, H (1966), *Orangeism in Ireland and Britain 1795–1836*, London, Routledge and Kegan Paul.

Sibbett, RM (1914), *Orangeism in Ireland and throughout the empire*, vol 1, Belfast, Henderson.

Freemasonry is discussed in a number of publications produced by the Grand Lodge of Ireland and in a number of local historical studies:

Crossle, F (1909), *A history of Nelson masonic lodge, no 16*, Newry, Newry.

Crossle, P (1973), *Irish masonic records*, Dublin, Grand Lodge of Ireland.

Lepper, JH and Crossle, P (1925), *History of the grand lodge of free and accepted masons of Ireland*, vol 1, Dublin, Lodge of Research.

McNeilly, DJM (1965), 'Masonic processions' in *Transactions for the years 1963–1968*, vol XV, Dublin, Lodge of Research.

Parkinson, RE (1957), *History of the grand lodge of free and accepted masons of Ireland*, vol 2, Dublin, Lodge of Research.

Simpson, WG (1924), *The history and antiquities of freemasonry in Saintfield, County Down*, Saintfield.

Simpson, WG (1926), *Masonry of the olden time in the Comber district*, Lisburn.

There have been few studies of the Ancient Order of Hibernians undertaken in recent years. The main ones are:

Foy, MT (1976), 'The AOH: an Irish politico-religious pressure group', unpublished MA thesis, Queen's University, Belfast.

Hepburn, AC (1996), *A past apart: studies in the history of Catholic Belfast, 1850–1950*, Belfast, Ulster Historical Foundation.

A small number of studies discuss the emergence and development of the trade unions in Ireland:

Boyd, A (1985), *The rise of the Irish trade unions*, Tralee, Anvill Press.

Boyle, J (1988), *The Irish labour movement in the nineteenth century*, Washington, Catholic University of America Press.

Morgan, A (1991), *Labour and partition: the Belfast working class 1905–1923*, London, Pluto Press.

O'Connor, E (1992), *A labour history of Ireland, 1824–1960*, Dublin, Gill and Macmillan.

The history and practices of the Orange Order are reasonably well documented, and there are a small number of studies of the Hibernians but the other marching orders are poorly documented. Buckley (1985–6) discusses the symbolism of the Royal Black Institution; Morgan (1991) has a chapter on the Independent Orange Order; and Fraser (forthcoming) has a chapter on the Apprentice Boys. I am not aware of any academic material on the Junior Orange Order, the Women's Orange Order or the Irish National Foresters. However, there are a growing number of publications and local histories produced by members of the various bodies although these are often difficult to find. A number of such recent publications can be found in the political collection of the Linen Hall Library in Belfast.

Besides these various publications a lot of historical details can be found in the newspapers and magazines. In particular the *Belfast News Letter*, which has been published since 1737, provides an opportunity to follow the development of parading practices from the beginning of the modern period. The *Northern Whig* and later the *Belfast Telegraph* and the *Irish News* also have regular reports and together these four papers provide a thorough but varied coverage of events. Other short-lived papers are worth consulting and sometimes produce interesting accounts of parades. Many local papers also offer more specific coverage of parades in their relevant areas. Finally, *The Orange Standard*, the monthly paper of the Orange Order, has regular articles on parades and frequently contains photographs of newly unfurled banners.

INDEX